Some Reviews

"If you want to be a person who radiates energy while 'working' any room and every situation—as well as your walk through life—Dr. Jerry Teplitz has written *Switched-On Living* for you."
— Susan Roane
Author, *How to Work a Room* and *The Secrets of Savvy Networking*

"*Switched-On Living* is filled with easy methods to show you how to draw strength and energy from your mind/body connection and integrate the hemispheres of your brain for better health, creativity and productivity. This book is must reading for anyone who has stress in his life—and that's just about all of us."
— Ken Dychtwald, Ph.D.
Author, *Bodymind* and *Age Wave*

"I highly recommend *Switched-On Living* to anyone who is interested in using his life energy efficiently and becoming healthier and happier in the future. The techniques shared in this book will also create very positive results almost instantly! This is information that is very necessary and should be taught in our schools."
— Lee Milteer
Author, *Feel & Grow Rich*

"Dr. Teplitz has written a highly readable book integrating old wisdom on the body's energy systems with modern research on whole-brain learning. He has woven this information into practical techniques for increasing physical wellness and vitality with mind power for high level performance in all areas of one's life."
— Lee Pulos, Ph.D.
Clinical Psychologist
Author, *Beyond Hypnosis*

"*Switched-On Living* combines simple, practical, and powerful tools to reduce stress and improve quality of life. I highly recommend Dr. Teplitz's book. It's required reading as well as a reference source."
— Ron L. Fronk, Ph.D.
Author, *The Turning Point Library*

"A fascinating book. I started reading it and couldn't put it down. I've already implemented one of its ideas in my office to improve productivity."
— Tony Alessandra, Ph.D.
Author, *People Smarts*

"Dr. Teplitz provides a variety of tools for throwing the switch toward health."
— C. Norman Shealy, M.D.
Founder, American Holistic Medical Association

"Jerry Teplitz amazes me. He is always expressing things others haven't even begun to wonder about. His new book, *Switched-On Living* will make you aware of factors that affect your life beyond common experience. Jerry is a teacher and practitioner who knows and who cares."
— Jim Cathcart
Past President, National Speakers Association
Author, *Relationship Selling*

"I am astonished how Educational Kinesiology techniques uncover imbalances in our physiology and simultaneously correct the difficulty and restore balance. Edu-K cuts effortlessly through much intellectual analysis and cloudy facades to reach deep-seated conflicts in our psychology and physiology. Through Edu-K, individuals gain mastery and self-responsibility toward understanding and resolving life's challenges. I heartily recommend Educational Kinesiology to all!"
— Paul Curlee, M.D.

"It is very difficult to be a dynamic success unless you feel well. Jerry Teplitz' book *Switched-On Living* is practical, livable, and an interesting read. His practical advice will help you put more into your living."
— Patricia Fripp
Author, *Get What You Want*
Past President, National Speakers Association

"*Switched-On Living* is an exciting new resource for people who want to improve the quality of their health and reduce their levels of stress immediately. A real eye-opener—I highly recommend it."
— Tolly Burkan, Founder
Firewalking Institute of Research and Education

"Years ago I loved a popular song entitled 'Body and Soul' but never understood how to link the two in order to increase my work production and life satisfaction. This magnificent book by Dr. Teplitz and Norma Eckroate brings the two elements together in such a simple-to-understand way that the techniques can be put to instant practical use. Is there anyone who does not need energy-boosting systems that truly work? For the first time, I have grasped exactly how to switch on the power of mind and body in order to accomplish more in my life and my business. I especially like the quick and easy 'Energy Enhancers' in this book. Bravo!"
—Dottie Walters
Author, *Speak and Grow Rich*

Switched-On Living

Easy Ways to Use the Mind / Body Connection to Energize Your Life

Jerry V. Teplitz, J.D., Ph.D.
with Norma Eckroate

Happiness Unlimited Publications
1304 Woodhurst Drive
Virginia Beach, VA 23454
Phone: 757 496-8008
FAX: 757 496-9955
E-MAIL: info@Teplitz.com
WEB SITE: www.Teplitz.com

Copyright © 1994, 2001
By Jerry V. Teplitz, JD, Ph.D., and Norma Eckroate

First trade paperback edition published 1994 by
Hampton Roads Publishing Co.

All rights reserved, including the right to reproduce this
work in any form whatsoever, without permission
in writing from the publisher, except for brief passages
in connection with a review.

The authors are indebted to Dr. John Diamond and Paul
Dennison, Ph.D. and the Educational Kinesiology
Foundation for use of material in this book
on Educational Kinesiology.

Illustrations by Cris Arbo
Kirlian photographs by Al Hulstrunk
Aura photographs by Gwen Kemp
Cover design by Lorraine Garnett
Cover at by Victor Bornia

If you are unable to order this book from your local
Bookseller, you may order directly from the publisher.
Quantity discounts for organizations are available.
Call 800 77-RELAX

ISBN 978-0-939372-02-7
Printed in the United States of America

This book is dedicated to my parents, Herb and Ceil, who, once they understood what I am doing, have been very supportive.

Contents

Chapter 1.
An Introduction to Switching-On / 11

Chapter 2.
Body Talk: Behavioral Kinesiology / 14
The Muscle Checking Method / 16
Why BK Checking Works / 19
Five Percenters and Over-Energized Individuals / 20
Surrogate BK Checking / 22

Chapter 3.
Switching-On Your Life Energy / 24
The Body's Energy Pathways: Meridian Lines / 24
The Body's Energy Field: The Aura / 26
The Energy Enhancers / 35
Energizing the World Around You / 48
A Word About Words / 49

Chapter 4.
The Brain Switch: Educational Kinesiology / 52
Brain Gym™ / 55
Educational Kinesiology Balancing For Goals / 58
Educational Kinesiology Muscle Checking / 61
Calibration or Pacing / 64
Self-Checking Methods / 69
Positive Living Action Balance / 71
Seven-Minute Tune-Up for a Switched-On Day / 73

Chapter 5.
Switching-On Your Diet / 78
Food Sensitivities / 78
Energizing Food / 79

Chapter 6.
Switching-On Your Environment / 85
Lighting / 85
Color / 92
Music / 94
Electromagnetic Fields from Power Lines, Computers,
Appliances, and Other Sources / 100
The Positive Side of Electricity / 102
The Work Environment / 103
Additional Environmental Factors / 107

Chapter 7.
Switching-On Your Day / 108

Appendix / 113
Product Suppliers
Associations and Foundations
Suggested Reading

Notes / 115

Acknowledgements

Gratitude and thanks to the following individuals:

John Diamond, M.D., whose work known as Behavioral Kinesiology became the basis of what I've been sharing with seminar audiences and through the media for the last 14 years;

Paul Dennison, Ph.D., and Gail Dennison, the creators of a revolutionary learning system called Educational Kinesiology, which has opened new vistas for me and my work;

Al Hulstrunk for his help in reviewing the Kirlian photography section of this book and for graciously allowing us to reproduce his Kirlian photos;

Gwen Kemp for letting us reprint the aura photography photo of herself;

Cris Arbo, whose illustrations bring concepts to life;

Bob Friedman, Frank DeMarco, Kathy Grotz, and everyone at Hampton Roads Publishing whose enthusiasm about this book warms an author's heart;

Pat Smith, for his great cover design;

Sandra Martin, whose encouragement and support are greatly appreciated.

Chapter 1

An Introduction to Switching-On

Have you ever noticed someone who walked into a crowded room and seemed to be radiating energy? The person who is "bubbling over" with energy is a person everyone notices. We're talking about an energy that carries you through your day with ease so that, at the end of the day, you're not falling into bed with exhaustion but still feeling good. Your sojourn in sleep is a restful and rejuvenating time. This is a switched-on person.

A switched-on person has energy to spare but can also attain a state of total relaxation in seconds. Unfortunately, that is not the way most people live. It is more common to find people who become exhausted during the day and can hardly make it to bedtime. At night many people toss and turn; even in sleep they can't truly relax. In fact, many people do not even know how to relax fully.

Truly being attuned to the sensitivities of the body involves an inner awareness that few have in our fast-paced society. To understand how we can easily access a switched-on lifestyle, I want to introduce you to the concept of the *energy body*. The scientific community has made a number of discoveries that prove the existence of this energy body which radiates in and through the physical body and even connects with our subconscious programming. In his book *The Body Electric*, Dr. Robert O. Becker refers to this inner connection as our body's "intricate and multilayered self-regulating feedback arrangement."[1]

In the new discipline called psychoneuroimmunology, researchers are proving an intricate connection between the mind and the body which relates to all aspects of the body's functioning, including health and healing, emotional well-being, and the immune system. In a now-classic pioneering study in psychoneuroimmunology, Stanford University School of Medicine researchers, Dr. George Solomon and Dr. Rudolf H. Moos, found that "...people who are genetically predisposed to arthritis but are emotionally healthy avert the disease."[2]

Summing up the study's proof of the strong link between the mind and body, Dr. Solomon said, "We assume from this that if you have the rheumatoid factor in your blood but stay in good condition psychologically, you won't get arthritis. On the other hand, if you're genetically predisposed, and endure long periods of anxiety and/or depression or suffer some major emotional upset, you are at a high risk of arthritis."[3]

We hear a lot today about the effects of stress on our bodies. There are untold multitudes of stresses bombarding our daily lives. And yet we can't go stick our heads in the sand in order to avoid stress. We have to live in the world. If, however, we identify the areas of our lives that are out of balance and switched-off, we'll be aware of some of the stresses in our own unique lifestyles. While there are many stresses out there in our world that we can't change, we *can* change some of them and we can change our susceptibility to many of the others.

In this book I'll share with you an easy way to identify stresses and, even more importantly, techniques for switching-on and balancing various aspects of life: from attitudes and beliefs to diet and even the music we listen to. Fortunately, it's easier than you'd think. Pioneers in the study of the body/mind connection have developed simple ways to do this.

We can divide the stresses that affect our body energy into three basic categories: environmental, psychological, and physiological. *Environmental* influences include the air we breathe, the music we hear, the lighting under which we live and work, and even the color of the walls in our homes and workplaces. *Psychological* influences include the way we are affected by our attitudes, beliefs, thoughts, and feelings.

Physiological influences include the effects of substances such as food, alcohol, and chemicals we ingest from sources such as our food and water supply; pesticides; household products such as air fresheners and fabric softeners; personal hygiene products such as deodorants, hand and body lotions, and hair colorings; cleaning compounds; and even chemical treatments on our lawns.

Last year I traveled to many cities and presented 90 seminars on stress management, leadership, and sales training to corporations, associations, and governmental agencies, both in the United States and abroad. That's a lot of plane flights, taxi rides, and packing of bags.

Since my job is teaching people how to manage and minimize the stresses in their lives, I have discovered many techniques which have prevented me from being totally burned out traveling. I know these techniques work from three standpoints: I use them myself; I've taught them to more than a million people and continue to receive their positive feedback; and convincing research has been conducted over a period of many years. These techniques may be completely new to you. Even though they might seem simple or unusual, I urge you to actively apply all the information in this book to your life. It's a wonderful feeling to have the power to be switched-on to living and achieving peak energy in your life.

We'll look at systems which work with our body energy, with integration of the left and right hemispheres of the brain, and aspects of our environment that we can switch-on. In the next chapter I'll share one of these systems, Behavioral Kinesiology, which will give you a picture of some new and exciting ideas.

Chapter 2

Body Talk: Behavioral Kinesiology

Can you identify the elements in your life which are stressful to you? It is possible to identify stresses by becoming sensitive to the way your body feels and the areas where you hold tension; few people, however, are attuned to their bodies to the degree necessary to identify stresses in this manner.

But what if you had an easy way to determine exactly what forces, external and internal, are stressful to you? It would be helpful, wouldn't it. As a matter of fact, there *is* a unique and simple way to do just that! It costs no money and it can be done anywhere. It will help you in identifying all the stresses in your life, and, even more importantly, it can be used to show you how to reduce those stresses. In this chapter, we'll see how this body-checking method can be used to show the body's ability to tell you which foods are good for you and which are not. In later chapters, I'll show you other ways to use this fascinating system to switch-on your daily life.

Since this body-checking involves applying physical pressure to your arm muscle, you'll need someone to participate with you. You don't have to be physically strong to do the check or to be checked. The key concept in the checking is that stimuli affect muscle strength. When you apply pressure on your partner's arm, her arm will remain strong when she is exposed to a positive stimulus; and her arm muscle will be weakened when she is exposed to a negative one. This will make more sense as you proceed further.

The name of this body-checking method is Behavioral

Kinesiology; it was developed by Dr. John Diamond, a psychiatrist. In his practice, Dr. Diamond became frustrated because many of his patients would initially get better and then would backslide. He realized that this occurred when they returned to the conditions in their lives that had caused or aggravated their problems in the first place. Since identifying those conditions wasn't easy, he searched for a way to determine what aspects of their lives were contributing to their illnesses.

Dr. Diamond finally found an answer in the principles of Applied Kinesiology, developed by Dr. George Goodheart, which uses muscle checking as a way of evaluating a person's physical health. Many chiropractors use Applied Kinesiology in their work today. Dr. Diamond believed that this same technique might work to isolate and help to alter stresses in his patients' lives. His research showed that the muscle-checking techniques used in Applied Kinesiology could indeed be used to determine stressful conditions in our lives. He named his technique Behavioral Kinesiology (BK) and introduced this breakthrough in his books, *Your Body Doesn't Lie* (also published under the title *BK: Behavioral Kinesiology*) and *Life Energy*.

The systems of both BK and Applied Kinesiology owe a debt to Dr. Robert Lovett of Harvard Medical School, who initially developed a muscle-checking system in 1912. Dr. Lovett's work was expanded in 1922 by Dr. Charles Lowman, an orthopedic surgeon, and again in 1936 by physical therapists Henry and Florence Randall. Unfortunately, just like other systems which don't easily fit in the Western scientific paradigm (such as acupuncture), muscle checking was never widely disseminated to the medical profession. Today, though, it is not uncommon to find customers in health food stores muscle checking various brands of nutritional supplements to find the one which is best for their body chemistry. Muscle checking may not yet be mainstream knowledge, but its effectiveness is clear to thousands of people who use it as an adjunct to their health maintenance on a regular basis.

As a professional speaker on stress management, I use this BK muscle-checking technique in my seminars. Audiences have found it amazing and exciting. I have conducted muscle checking on hundreds of thousands of people, including presidents of corporations, top government officials, office workers, sales personnel, homemakers, and students. Everyone receives a first-hand experience with this amazing technique because I have all my audiences participate and do the muscle checking on each other.

BK muscle checking is something you must experience in order to believe, so now you need to find someone to be your partner. By following these instructions, you will soon discover for yourself the amazing ability your body has to simply and easily tell you what it finds positive and beneficial and what it finds negative and detrimental.

The Muscle-Checking Method

Read through these instructions for BK checking first, and then follow them on your partner. It is extremely important for you to do the muscle checking now in order to understand this concept as it appears throughout the book.

BK Check: Finding Normal Resistance

1. Face your partner.

2. Your partner should raise one arm up from the side of the body so it is at a right angle to the body and level with the shoulder, with the thumb pointing toward the floor. Imagine a bird with a wing outstretched, and you'll have the correct arm position. The other arm should remain at the side of the body.

3. Now place one of your hands on your partner's extended arm, just above the wrist. Place your other hand on your partner's opposite shoulder.

4. Instruct your partner to resist as you push down, firmly and steadily with a hard pressure, on the extended arm. Say out loud, "Ready—resist," as you are about to push down on your partner's arm. You are not trying to

force her arm down; her arm should stay fairly level during the pressure; however, you want to place a hard, steady pressure on the arm in order to measure her normal level of resistance. You should press firmly for several seconds, and then release.

Finding Normal Resistance.

I call this checking *in neutral.* It is important to check a person in neutral before doing any other checking so you can determine her normal level of resistance.

Note: If you push her arm down more than an inch or two, you have pushed through her ability to resist. Press again with a bit less pressure. Always follow this concept of checking in neutral to check a person's level of resistance. Just remember to exert pressure based on the person's level of strength. For example, you would press harder when you are muscle checking a super-strong football player and more gently if you are muscle checking a petite person.

Now you are ready to do a BK muscle-checking procedure. We'll start with a check on various food items.

BK Muscle-Checking Procedure

Before you begin, collect one or two items from each group below:

Group A:
- a small packet of sugar (or put a teaspoon of sugar in a napkin and fold it up)
- a small packet of artificial sweetener made of saccharin (such as Sweet 'n' Low)
- a candy bar

Group B:
- a nut such as an almond or cashew
- a piece of fruit such as a grape or an apple
- a piece of celery or carrot

1. Ask your partner to put her arm out, thumb down. Place one of the gathered items in her hand by the side of her body.

2. Tell her to resist as you press down on her arm.

3. Repeat with each of the items, keeping track of the results especially as to which items checked weak.

4. Switch roles and have your partner check you.

Lowered Resistance.

Checking Strong.

On almost everyone I've checked, the items in Group A—sugar, artificial sweetener, and candy—will be weakening, and the items in Group B—nuts, fruits, and vegetables—will be strengthening. If you checked weak on any of the Group B items, you may have a food sensitivity, which is discussed further in Chapter 5.

Sugar is an example of a substance that has a negative impact on the body, and the body knows it! The reason sugar is detrimental is because it is absorbed too rapidly into the bloodstream for the body to process it. This results in an excessively high blood-sugar level. The body, to protect itself, secrets insulin to reduce the sugar level. The BK checking indicates that sugar has a negative impact on the body's energy field. It is depleting rather than vitalizing to the body. Sugar is discussed in greater detail in Chapter 5.

Why BK Checking Works

Now that you have experienced BK checking, let me explain *why* it works. Your body is a complex organism that is programmed to strive for wellness. It has an incredible intelligence and an ability to respond to the unique ways you program it.

You may have noticed that when your partner held an unhealthy food you had to put less pressure on her arm for it to go down. Conversely, when your partner held a healthy item, you could apply much greater pressure on the arm but it still remained very strong.

The actual muscle group we are body checking is the deltoid muscle. When you are doing the checking procedure and the arm goes down easily, the deltoid muscle signifies that the entire body's energy level is in a weakened and switched-off state. When the arm stays up, it indicates that the person's energy is strong and switched-on. While you can do the BK checking on other muscles in your body such as the leg muscles, we use the deltoid because it is more conveniently located.

If, during the muscle checking, the person's arm becomes tired, you can simply switch to the other arm. Just be sure to check the "new" arm first for its normal level of resistance before you begin any further checking.

If a person is not weakened by some of the Group A items, re-check them. If you re-check and that person is still strong on a particular item, there are a couple possibilities as to why this is occurring.

One possibility is that the person's body is okay with that substance. She may have eliminated the substance from her diet so the body no longer recognizes it when held in the hand. First, have the person put the substance in her mouth and re-check. If her arm comes down, then she really is sensitive to the substance. If her arm still stays up, there are two possibilities to consider.

Five Percenters and Over-Energized Individuals

If you followed the body-checking steps correctly and your arm did not go down on the Group A items, you are either a *Five Percenter* or *Over-Energized.*

Five Percenters are so named because less than five percent of the population remains switched-on in almost all BK checking. Their arms don't go down because they don't seem to be weakened by the same negative stimuli that weaken most people. These people are functioning at high energy levels, so when the usual daily stresses come up, they are able to effectively deal with them without being weakened.

When you muscle check people in the other category, Over-Energized Individuals, they also check strong on everything, just like Five Percenters, but they are giving inaccurate readings. It appears that these individuals have overactive adrenal glands that are operating on a continuous basis and not shutting off. In other words, these people are in constant states of the fight-or-flight response, which override all the systems of the body.

There is a way to determine if someone is Over-Energized or is a true Five Percenter. Just for a moment, turn to the Thymus Level Check on page 41 and do Steps 1 and 2. If his arm stays up, it indicates he is either a true Five Percenter or is Over-Energized. To determine which it is, have the person tap the fleshy part of the side of one hand (located just below the pinkie finger) against the same area on the other hand about 35 times. (See *Illustration* .) Believe it or not, that action seems to shut the adrenal glands down at least for a while. Then do the Thymus Level Check again. If the person is a Five Percenter, his arm will stay up. If he is Over-Energized, his arm will come down and he will give appropriate responses in all further muscle checking. A person who is Over-Energized can do this simple exercise a couple times a day to help himself calm down.

*Tap the fleshy part of the side of one hand
(located just below the pinky finger) against the same area
on the other hand about 35 times.*

Remember, too, that some people have sensitivities to certain foods or substances that most of us can tolerate. One day at a seminar, I was demonstrating the BK checking. I checked a man on an almond that had been placed in a sealed envelope. He didn't know what he was holding. Since almonds are a nutritious food, his arm should have stayed up. But, to my surprise, his arm went down. I knew something was wrong but I didn't know what. I explained to the audience what had taken place and told them this was unusual because normally a person's arm is weakened when muscle checked on a positive food such as an almond only if the person has a food sensitivity to almonds. As I explained this, the man standing behind me said that he has an allergy to almonds. The muscle checking had accurately indicated that almonds are weakening to his system.

You can take this checking procedure one step further if you wish and put the items in Groups A and B in sealed envelopes and mix them up. Then go through the checking procedure with each envelope. When you open the envelopes, you will find that the results are the same. Even though you and the person being muscle checked do not know which envelopes contain "positive" items, and which contain "negative" items, the body still accurately reads the items and responds accordingly. As the title of Dr. John Diamond's pioneering book on this subject so aptly puts it, *Your Body Doesn't Lie.*

As I'll share throughout the book, you can also use BK checking to determine the impact of other foods, music, lighting, and, in fact, anything in your environment to identify its effect on you.

Surrogate BK Checking

BK muscle checking can also be done even if the person does not have the physical strength or is ill and cannot resist the pressure by enlisting the help of another person who will act as a surrogate. Ask the person being checked to hold the substance and have the surrogate touch the person being checked as you muscle check the surrogate's arm resistance. (If you are doing surrogate muscle checking for someone who is unable to hold the substance, such as an infant, simply place it on his body while the surrogate's arm resistance is checked.) A weakness in the surrogate's arm muscles will indicate that the item being tested is not recommended for the person, while a strong arm muscle indicates that it is an appropriate choice. Surrogate muscle checking can be done for people who are extremely ill, infants, small children, and pets.

Chapter 3

Switching-On Your Life Energy

Now that you've tried the Behavioral Kinesiology muscle checking, you may have some questions, such as: How does it work? How can a food affect my arm strength? This chapter will answer these questions for you.

The Body's Energy Pathways: Meridian Lines

While this information may be new to you, the basis for these concepts has been around for thousands of years. First, let's look at the concept of acupuncture. Western medicine has confirmed that the Oriental healing system of acupuncture, which was developed over 5,000 years ago, works and its use in the United States continues to spiral upward. This system, which is in many ways contrary to the principles of Western medicine, is so effective that thousands of traditional medical doctors are also becoming acupuncturists—some traveling to China to learn the art.

One example of the amazing power of acupuncture to stimulate the body's own natural healing mechanisms is the fact that it activates the body's production of the natural pain-killers, endorphins, at a level that is 200 times more powerful than morphine.

Acupuncture is based on the existence of energy pathways running through and around the body. These pathways are called *meridian lines*. To understand this concept more clearly, think of your body's central nervous system as a series of buried telephone cables transporting messages throughout the body. Now think of the meridian lines as communication towers relaying signals to each other. A message is sent from one to the other without anyone seeing or feeling the signal. The meridian lines are points in the body that transfer these energy messages around the body; the transfer is done at the speed of light. The important point for us to remember is that *there is a correlation between the amount of energy being transmitted through the body and how switched-on and stress-free we are.*

Scientists have been able to measure these lines by locating unique differences in electrical resistance at the exact places on the body where the ancient acupuncturists mapped out these points.

When you start the day feeling great, your meridian lines are bubbling over with energy. The opposite is also true: when you start the day feeling tired or negative, you will have low vitality. You will seem to have hardly any energy at all. Your meridian flow is inhibited. Remember how you felt at the end of a day that was negative.

Research has proven that you can actually change your meridian-line energy instantly, uplifting and strengthening it. Later in this chapter, I'll share seven ways to do just that; I call these methods the *Energy Enhancers.*

According to acupuncture theory, there are twelve major meridian lines running through your body. Almost all of these meridian lines relate to different organs, muscles, and nerve groupings in the body. For example, there is a spleen meridian line, a stomach line, a kidney line, etc. The energy flows continuously but at varying levels of intensity through these lines.

When a person's energy is unbalanced or blocked at a particular point in the meridian system, the organs, muscles, and nerves connected to that particular system will not function optimally. If the blockage is extensive enough, the decrease in vitality can result in illness or suboptimal health.

BK muscle checking is a way to measure the effect of various stimuli on the body's meridian system. If the arm is weak and goes down easily, then we know that a meridian line is being adversely affected by that particular stimuli—be it a food, thought, piece of music, or substance in the person's environment.

To put it simply, anything that *reduces* and switches off our energy decreases the body's ability to handle stress effectively. Anything that *uplifts* and switches on our energy increases the level of stress the body can process.

The Body's Energy Field: The Aura

You may be skeptical about the results of the BK muscle-checking procedures. After all, how does the body know that the substance held in the hand is positive or negative? The answer to that question relates to what is called the invisible energy field or *aura* which surrounds the entire body. Measuring the aura is another way of determining the immediate impact every time a negative or positive stimulus influences your body energy.

The existence of the energy field surrounding the body was demonstrated in the 1940s by a process called Kirlian effect photography. Kirlian photography is very simple. A person places a part of his body, such as a finger, on a photographic plate; then a high-frequency electrical charge is put through the plate and a photograph is made. The photograph reveals that the body seems to be made of constantly changing colored lights which appear in patterns resembling flares or clouds. This detectable auric envelope surrounding the body extends varying distances. On most individuals it extends several inches; on some high-energy people it can extend a number of feet.

Every object, either animate or inanimate, has an aura. However, the energy field of an animate subject (such as a person or a leaf) tends to be more complex, vibrant, and variable than the energy field of an inanimate subject (such as a piece of furniture). The size, shape, and color of a person's aura changes dramatically and immediately to reflect what the person is doing, thinking, or feeling. It will also reflect his state of health. In addition to still photographs, motion pictures can now be made using corona photography, allowing us to see these changes in the aura.

Through Kirlian photography we can see that plant life has these energies, too. A leaf on a plant has an aura around it; when the leaf is pulled off the branch, the aura will continue to be visible for a period of time, ranging from minutes to several hours. The size of the energy band around the leaf will gradually decrease as the leaf withers. (See *Illustration.*)

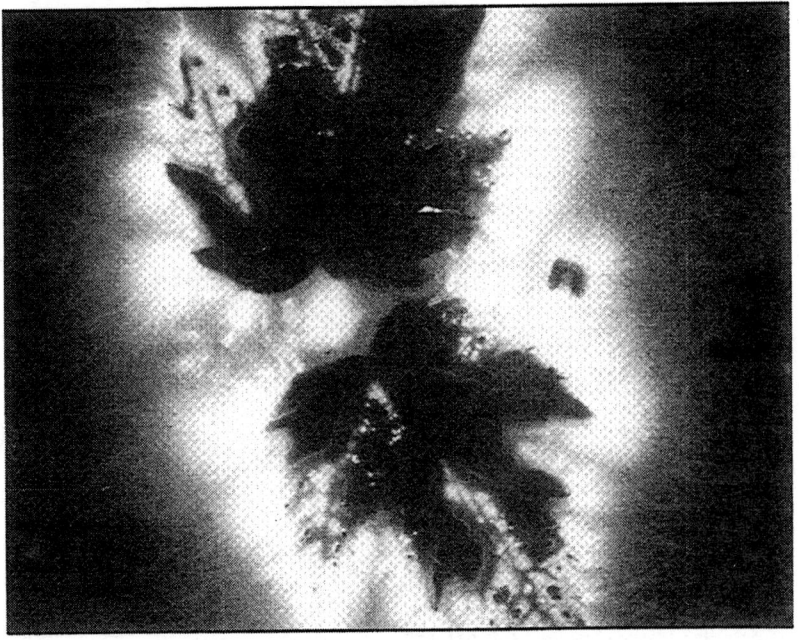

Energy band surrounding a maple leaf.

The Kirlian process demonstrates that *everything* emanates, and is surrounded by, these energy bands. The mild electrical charge used in the photographic process enhances this invisible energy in the same way that sunlight streaming through the window allows us to see tiny dust particles in the air. Until the sunlight shines on these floating dust particles, they are invisible to our eyes.

The Kirlian photos of a fingertip show very different auras

for a person having loving thoughts and the same person having angry thoughts. (See *Illustrations below*.)

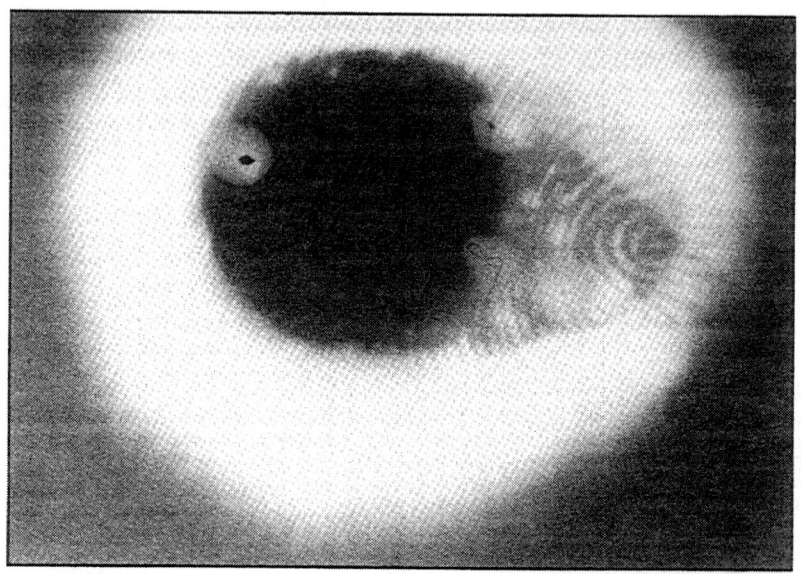

Kirlian photo of a fingertip of a person while having loving thoughts.

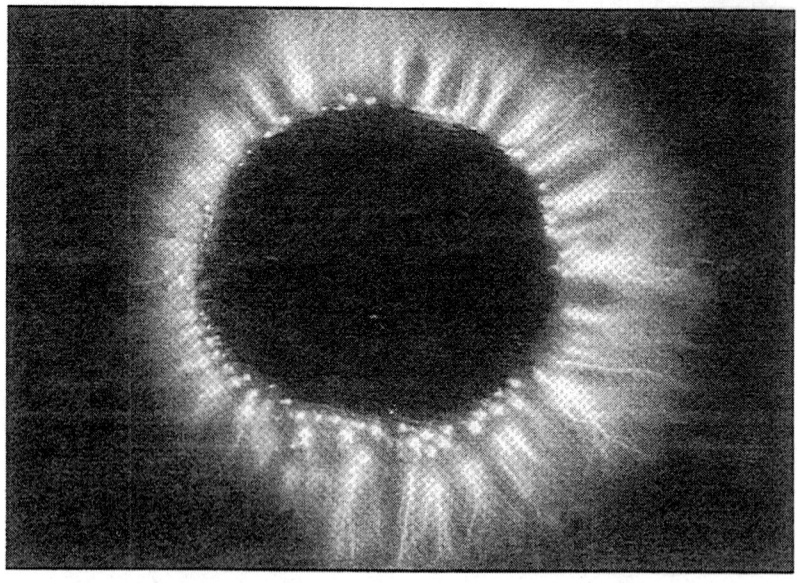

Kirlian photo of a fingertip of a person while having angry thoughts.

Aura photography is another method which confirms the existence of an energy band around the body. It involves placing one's hand on a metal plate. Then a slight electrical charge is put through the plate; this electrical charge is sent to a computer which analyzes it as it scans the person's electromagnetic energy field. The computer program uses the acupuncture meridians to identify the vibrational rates and frequencies within the body and then translates these frequencies into the resulting "aura photo."

Researchers of aura photography have found that this process replicates the aura just as it is seen by highly sensitive people who are able to actually see auras. Different people's aura photographs show how their energy bands differ in size, shape, and color.

Gwen Kemp, an expert in both Kirlian and aura photography, has shared the aura photo of herself in the illustration below. You'll notice a patch of light on the right in Gwen's photo. An aura photo of me is shown on the next page. In my photo, the light evenly surrounds my face. If these photos were reprinted in color, you'd see that each person's aura photograph has different colors—sometimes a number of colors in the same photo.

Aura photo of Gwen Kemp.

30 / SWITCHED-ON LIVING

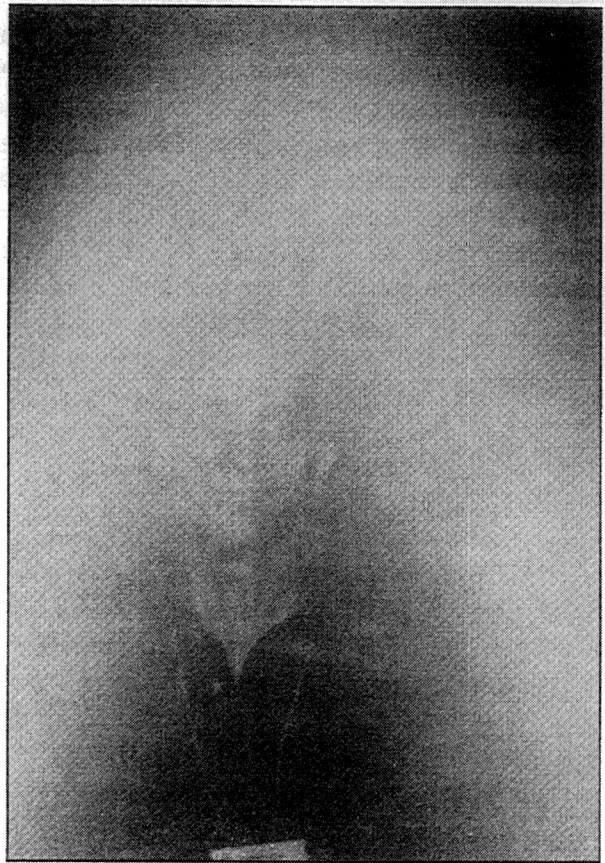

Aura photo of Jerry Teplitz.

Another analogy helpful to understanding auras is a television set that isn't hooked up to cable. The signals coming from the television station to our TVs at home are all around us. We are just not aware of them because our bodies cannot receive those signals. It takes the TV antenna and the wiring of the TV for us to "see" the picture being transmitted. A Japanese soldier from World War II was found on a deserted island thirty years after the war had ended. When he first saw a television, he asked how they got the people inside the box. Similarly, for the average person it's difficult to understand how a cellular phone can allow us to make a phone call to someone halfway around the world with no connection to wires. Even though the history of muscle checking stretches back to 1912, for most of us this is brand-new information. Kirlian photography and aura photography, although not yet accessible to the average person, prove that every living thing has an aura.

You might also want to think of your aura as the body's "sixth sense." I'm sure you have experienced yourself working busily on a project when suddenly you had the feeling someone was right behind you. When you turned around, you found that your sense was correct. It is this "sixth sense" which gives you the ability to "know" when someone walks into the room, even if you don't see or hear anyone. When he gets close enough to you, you "feel" his aura touching yours.

Some people can actually perceive the aura surrounding others. However, since most of us cannot, the BK muscle checking is a way to determine how things coming into your sphere of influence are affecting you. It gives you the information you need to reduce the impact of negative stimuli and increase the positive.

Now let's look at another aspect of the meridian lines. The meridian lines run in specific pathways along the body, and they travel or move in specific directions. When you make a movement along the body *in the direction in which the line runs*, you are *adding* to body energy. A movement in the opposite direction, however, is weakening. You could think of this in terms of rowing upriver against the current and downriver with the current. Going against the current makes your body work very hard. When you row with the current, you move very quickly and easily to your destination.

Certain actions which we do every day are going "against the current." When you make any movement that is against the natural flow of the energy, you are decreasing your life energy. We refer to this as *cutting* the meridian pathway.

Find a friend and do this muscle check, and then I'll give you some simple ways to counteract these cuts in your body's energy.

Stomach Meridian Check

1. Do the BK check for Normal Resistance.

2. While your partner keeps her arm extended, use one of your hands to trace a straight line, from her eye to her foot, down the same side of her body, without touching her body at all.

3. Immediately check the resistance in her arm by telling her to resist as you push down. Her arm should go down easily. Cutting the line has briefly switched off her energy.

4. Have your partner extend her arm again. This time, trace a line from her foot to her eye, without touching her at all.

5. Immediately re-check your partner's ability to resist. You will find her checking strong again. You have now increased her energy flow and she is switched-on.

6. Have your partner check you.

Almost all people check weak when the line is traced downward, from the eye to the foot, because that motion is cutting the stomach meridian line. Then, when the line is traced in the opposite direction, from the foot to the eye, they check strong because that particular meridian line runs upward. Tracing a line in the direction the line naturally runs is strengthening to that particular meridian line and to the entire body. When you trace this meridian line upward from the foot to the eye, you are following the direction in which it flows, and you are strengthening both that meridian line and the entire body. By moving in ways that go with your line's flow, instead of against it, you wind up actually strengthening your body.

Let's check for the spleen meridian line.

Spleen Meridian Check

1. Check again for Normal Resistance.

2. With your hand by your partner's arm at the level he would wear a belt, trace a line without touching his body from the side of the body to the area of the belly button. It's just a short stroke.
3. Immediately check his resistance, and his extended arm should go down easily. His energy is switched off.

4. To strengthen the spleen line again, you will need to do a massage along the line you traced with your hand. Move your hand along the belt from the side of the body to the belly button area, massaging briefly. You must actually touch the person this time.

5. Immediately re-check your partner's resistance. His arm will stay strong and switched-on.

When you first traced along the spleen meridian line without touching, you went against its natural flow, weakening it and the entire energy system of the body. An awareness of these *energy cuts* may be more practical than you think. For example, a common activity in which you do this movement is ironing clothes. Think about it. You are cutting your spleen meridian line each time you move the iron. No wonder most people find ironing so tiring. Later in this chapter I will tell you a way to combat this problem so you can have pressed clothes and not cut your spleen meridian every time you move the iron.

You can demonstrate the effects of ironing clothing with a partner. Do three or four movements as if you were ironing and then ask your partner to muscle check you immediately afterwards. Surprise, surprise—your arm will go down. You can correct the effects of this by massaging yourself as in Step 4 above and then asking your partner to re-check you to demonstrate that your energy has now returned. To prevent this effect from occurring in the first place, use the Second Energy Enhancer, which I'll cover shortly.

These meridian lines are easily cut many times during the course of a normal day. If you pass people in the hallway and they move their arms in front of your midsection without touching, they have actually cut your spleen meridian line. Keep in mind that normally when this happens your body will readjust its energy balance. However, since these cuts may be happening all day long, they add to the pile-up of stresses and can leave the body fatigued and unable to quickly and effectively re-balance the system.

Many workers in factories, restaurants, and offices are depleting their energy with every move they make because the height of their work counters causes them to cut the spleen meridian over and over. A simple adjustment of the counter height to a higher level so the spleen meridian line is not influenced can make all the difference in the workers' vitality and attitude. We're all much cheerier when we are feeling vital and healthy. Corporations with whom I have worked are beginning to learn from techniques such as BK checking that small adjustments in heights add to productivity and even cut down on absenteeism. As I'll discuss later, other factors such as the type of lighting and the color of walls can also be changed with very favorable results that translate in increased corporate profits as well as increased employee health levels and job satisfaction.

A friend of mind, upon attending one of my seminars, became aware that every time he worked out with his barbells he was cutting the stomach meridian lines. (There are two of them, running from each foot to the eye above.) When he lifted the barbells from the floor to the ceiling, he was *strengthening* this meridian, and every time he lowered the barbells, he was *weakening* himself. After this was pointed out to him he began a variation on the routine. While he would keep the barbells close to his body on the upstroke, he would move his arms outward slightly past and to the sides of his body for the downstroke.

Before he made the change, his workouts were "going against the current." The positive energies were negated by the weakening downward movements. The particular muscles being worked were stronger due to the workout, but the overall result was no gain in body energy. After the simple change in his method, he reported an immediate improvement. He was able to exercise longer, did more repetitions, lifted more weight, and felt his workout was easier. By making this simple change in the way he moved, he increased his overall vitality and body energy, allowing him to exercise more vigorously and effectively.

Think of the specific movements you make in a day. When you move in certain directions, you may be cutting your meridian lines and thereby reducing your energy level. With some movements you will be able to make a simple adjustment, as my friend did in his workout, to change a depleting movement into a strengthening one. However, there are probably other movements you will not be able to change. Don't despair. There are other ways that you can use to keep your energy up while doing a "weakening" movement.

The Energy Enhancers

The *Energy Enhancers* will enable you to take control of your energy and boost it at will. They are amazingly simple and take only a few minutes; however, if you follow them you will notice the difference in your overall vitality and attitude.

Your First Energy Enhancer—
The Meridian Line Strengthener

To reduce fatigue, several times during the day simply trace a line from your foot to your eye on the same side of the body. You can do this while standing or sitting. Do this whenever you are beginning to feel tired. See if you don't notice a difference.

Your Second Energy Enhancer—The Energy Button

Another way to combat the effects of the meridian line cuts on your energy body—and to negate other stresses during the course of the day—is through using your *energy button*. The energy button is a place on the roof of your mouth, about a quarter-inch behind your front teeth, which connects the circuitry in your system. By holding your tongue gently up against the roof of your mouth at this spot, you are connecting and activating the body's internal circuitry. Your body's energy will continue to flow without being dissipated by the everyday activities that can cause you stress.

As strange as it may sound, simply holding your tongue in this position really works! It will increase your energy and vitality. As to exactly how it works, that still needs more research; however, through checking hundreds of thousands of people in seminars I've conducted over the years, I know it does work. The way I look at it, there are many medications which work even though medical science has no idea why or how. The same concept applies here—if it works, it works. If you gently hold your tongue to the roof of your mouth, you will have more energy at the end of the day.

To find out for yourself, let's now muscle check the energy button. Find a partner again to do this check.

MUSCLE CHECK OF THE ENERGY BUTTON

1. Check your partner's arm for Normal Resistance.

2. Give your partner a packet of sugar to hold and check her arm again. Her arm should go down easily.

3. Tell your partner to place her tongue gently against the roof of her mouth, about one quarter-inch behind the teeth.

4. Have your partner keep the tongue up while she is holding the sugar. Check her again. Her arm should stay up and switched-on as long as the tongue stays up.

5. While your partner has her tongue up, check again; while you are pressing, tell her quickly to take her tongue away from the roof of her mouth. Her arm should then go down.

6. Switch and have your partner do the check on you.

As with most people, your arm stays strong when you hold your tongue against the roof of your mouth, and as soon as you bring the tongue down, the negative effect of the sugar returns. You could also perform this muscle check with the stomach meridian line cutting check. When the tongue is up, you can't cut a meridian line.

To negate many of the stress effects you experience, simply develop the habit of keeping your tongue at the roof of your mouth all the time except, of course, when you are eating or talking. Remind yourself periodically to do this over the next few days, and you'll find that your tongue will take this position without any additional conscious effort on your part. After you become accustomed to the "up" position, you will find that keeping your tongue in the "down" position feels unusual.

As I mentioned, keeping the tongue up also keeps your meridian lines from being cut and weakened. Many athletes have shared with me the positive impact this technique has had on their performances. Just as the weight lifter increased his strength by changing his hand position on the downward movement of the barbells, you can use this Energy Button to negate the effects of weakening movements.

Whenever you iron clothing, type at a computer, do cleaning chores such as vacuuming or dusting, or write at a desk, you are cutting the spleen meridian line, so use the tongue-up position and see if your energy doesn't stay higher throughout this task.

Here's another movement to check using the Energy Button:

TENNIS STROKE MUSCLE CHECKING

1. Check your partner for Normal Resistance.

2. Have your partner use the same arm you just checked and ask him to go through the motions of three tennis forehand strokes. Now check his ability to resist. He will check strong and switched-on.

3. Have your partner do three backhand strokes with the same arm, and check again. He will now check weak and switched-off.

4. Ask your partner to put his tongue against the roof of his mouth, about a quarter-inch behind the teeth. Have him hold this position while he does the three backhand strokes again. Check him again. He will be strong and switched-on this time.

5. Have your partner check you, repeating Steps 1 through 4.

Step 2: Forehand strokes. *Step 3: Backhand strokes.*

As you can see and experience, different movements of the body have different effects on our energy system. The forehand movement was strengthening and the backhand weakening. The reason for the weakening effect of the backhand stroke is that it is a type of movement that causes *switching,* an unbalancing of the signals between the left and right hemispheres of the brain.

Switching produces a confusion in the body, resulting in stress and a weakening of energy. Among the other body movements that can switch a person are typical jumping jacks, in which arm and leg movements mirror each other exactly. This kind of movement is called *homolateral.* Any movement in which the arm and leg on the same side of the body move in unison will weaken the system. Doing jumping jacks differently, starting with the arms together above the head while the legs are apart, turns it into a *heterolateral* movement. This movement does not switch our brain hemispheres and, thus, is not weakening. Also, the tongue at the roof of the mouth will prevent the homolateral movement from weakening the body.

I suggested the tongue-up technique to a bicycle racer who was skeptical about it. Shortly afterwards, he was in a race and became tired, so he decided to put his tongue up. He went on to win the race! Another man, a middle-aged runner who competes in five-mile races, noticed a marked improvement in his racing time and the ease of running after he started keeping his tongue up all the time. And I've also had lots of feedback from golfers. One reported driving the ball 35 yards farther just by keeping his tongue up. Others have reported they are able to drive balls much, much farther than they ever did before.

Your Third Energy Enhancer—The "Okay" Sign

When you keep the tips of your index finger and thumb together (on either hand) to form a circle similar to an "okay" gesture, you are enhancing your energy. As when you use the tongue-up position, your inner circuitry is connected when you do this. (Touching any of the other fingers together will not give an energy-boosting impact.) You can place your hand anywhere, even in a pocket, and when you do the "okay" sign it will have the same result.

You can muscle check the impact of this yourself. Touch the tips of your index finger and thumb together and have someone do the Stomach Meridian Check and the Spleen Meridian Check on you. This "okay" sign will actually counteract the weakening effects of cutting those meridian lines. On the other hand, if you hold the tips of any of the other fingers together, you will find your energy system being weakened.

Your Fourth Energy Enhancer—The Thymus Thump

Once thought by the medical profession to become useless as we age, we now know the thymus gland is the body's center of immunity and resistance. It "trains" white blood cells (lymphocytes), called T cells, to fight infection and sends out hormones to help direct the activity of these T cells throughout the body.

Dr. John Diamond believes that the thymus gland regulates the flow of energy through the meridian pathways of the body. This means, in addition to defending the body from illness, the thymus is also charged with repairing the effects of stress and keeping us healthy. Therefore, as your meridian lines are being cut, the thymus automatically reestablishes the energy flow back along those cut lines. As the end of the day approaches, this readjustment process takes longer and longer to accomplish. Each incident of stress we experience increases the necessary recovery time. The more stresses we have in our lives, the harder it is to recover from each successive stressful event. For these reasons, most people are exhausted at the end of the day.

There is a way to immediately change this weakening effect. I call it the *Thymus Thump*. By tapping on the thymus gland, you can increase the thymus level of activity. This will result in a noticeable increase in overall energy and vitality.

The thymus gland is located in the center of the chest just below the collar bone, where the second button on a shirt is found. You can feel a slight bump there. Let's now check for thymus activity.

THYMUS LEVEL CHECK

1. Check your partner for Normal Resistance.

2. Ask your partner to place several fingers of the hand not being checked on the thymus spot, touching the body where the second button on a shirt is located. Check for resistance.

3. If she checks weak, have her tap or thump the thymus spot firmly ten to fifteen times with her fingertips. Then ask her to rest her fingers on the thymus spot again, and check the arm for resistance. The arm should now be strong and switched-on.

4. Have your partner do this check on you.

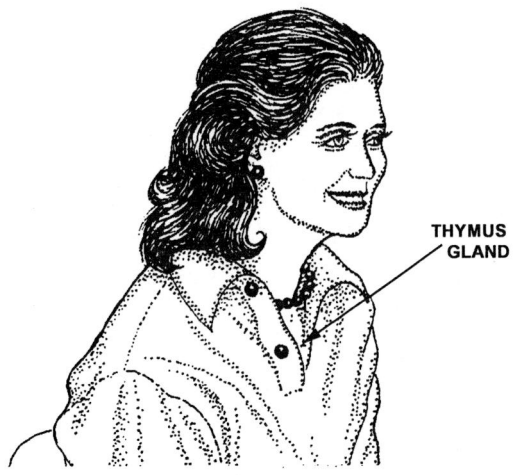

This is the location of the thymus gland.

The Thymus Thump automatically stimulates the thymus gland and dramatically raises the body's energies. If you do this routinely, five or six times a day, you will be better able to handle short-term stresses. The length of time the thymus will stay strong after doing the Thymus Thump varies with each person and with the stressful situations encountered. The more stresses, the less time the benefit will last.

In addition to the Thymus Thump, another very simple way to strengthen the thymus is to muscle check the person while he thinks about something very, very positive. His arm will check strong while he focuses on positive thoughts.

Your Fifth Energy Enhancer—Positive Thinking

I'm sure you've heard a great deal about the power of positive thinking. Let's do a muscle-checking procedure to show just how powerful your thoughts really are.

We will use an experience from your past in the following check; however, keep in mind that this technique can be used to determine the impact of *any* event in your life. Be prepared for some very amazing results.

MUSCLE CHECK FOR POSITIVE VERSUS NEGATIVE THOUGHTS

1. Check your partner for Normal Resistance.

2. While your partner keeps her arm extended, ask her to close her eyes and think of a negative past experience. Have her nod her head when she has this thought firmly pictured or felt in her mind. Then tell her to resist while you press down. She will be switched-off and her arm will go down easily, even though she resists with all her might.

3. Now tell your partner to resume the arm-extended position while thinking of a positive experience in her past. Again, ask her to close her eyes and nod her head when she is focused on this image. Then tell her to resist as you push down. She will now be switched-on; her arm will stay level and strong. It may feel even stronger than when you first checked her for normal resistance.

4. Switch roles and have your partner check you.

Your energy is being raised as long as you maintain the positive thought. It can be helpful for you to pick a very positive thought and use that thought as a "homing" device. Whenever you are fearful, worrying, or experiencing stress, focus your thoughts on this "homing" thought as a way to bring yourself back from the negative thoughts you are having. If you are thinking positive thoughts, it's very hard to be negative.

When you are running the negative thought through your mind—be it fear, anger, frustration, envy, jealousy, guilt, or worry—you are causing yourself stress and diminishing your strength, energy level, and resistance. You are even reducing the white corpuscle count in your blood. If you maintain these thoughts with enough intensity, they may make you more susceptible to disease and illness. These negative thoughts are depleting your body's energy reserves, and you are asking your body to work overtime to cope with the situation.

This concept does not mean that you should repress or ignore negative thoughts and feelings. Suppression is not the answer either because you will be internalizing the negativity if you just pretend it doesn't exist. Internalizing these emotions can even lead to illness. Instead, if you recognize, accept, and attempt to understand your feelings, you are in a better position to express them appropriately. In Chapter 4, I'll show you the Positive Living Action Balance as a way to actually get rid of, in two minutes, the negativity attached to the thoughts.

When you take a step back from your feeling and look at it objectively as though it belonged to someone else, you may be able to reduce the strength of the feeling so you can look at *why* you had that emotion. This objectivity will also allow you to change or accept the situation that caused the upsetting emotion in the first place.

Positive thoughts have the reverse effect; they strengthen the thymus gland. In fact, our entire energy body is strengthened whenever we have thoughts of love. In his book *Your Body Doesn't Lie*, Dr. John Diamond gives many examples of outward expressions of love, such as a smile or the physical posture of giving someone a hug, which are strengthening to the thymus. If this hugging embrace gesture is made toward a frightened child or someone who is troubled, it will instantly strengthen the recipient's thymus. This action is also beneficial to the person who is making the gesture. If you are under stress, simply thinking about hugging someone with love will strengthen your body energy. By raising your energy, you will lift the energy of everyone around you.

Here's a BK muscle check to change negative thoughts:

MUSCLE CHECK TO CHANGE NEGATIVE THOUGHTS

1. Check your partner for Normal Resistance.

2. Ask your partner to close her eyes and visualize a negative experience in her mind. Muscle check her. Her arm will go down. Then ask her to switch the negative experience and find something about it to view positively. However she defines it is fine.

3. Ask her to shake her head to indicate that she has made the switch.

4. Tell her to resist while you press down on her arm. Her arm will remain strong and switched-on.

This muscle check shows us once again the incredible power of the mind. By taking charge of a negative experience and simply *changing your mind* about how you view it, you can alter the impact the negative experience is having on you. All you need to do is to *decide* to think positively about the experience.

This understanding doesn't mean you're never going to have another stressful experience or negative thought; everyone does. I, too, have negative or stressful thoughts when things don't go the way I want them to. However, I know that I don't have to let those thoughts keep affecting me. I know I can instantly alter my thoughts about that negative experience and switch it to a positive view.

When you do this body checking, you may experience some initial difficulty changing a thought from negative to positive. In that case, you can think about a beautiful vacation spot or a happy experience from your past and that thought will eliminate the effects of a negative thought.

Your Sixth Energy Enhancer—The Energy Bubble

By now I hope it is clear that your thoughts have a great deal to do with your overall vitality and energy. What if there were a way to simply and easily protect yourself from the weakening effects of substances and thoughts simply by *thinking it so?* Well, there is. You can literally imagine an *energy bubble* surrounding your entire body. Just think it, and it's there.

Just say to yourself, silently or aloud, "My body is surrounded with a protective bubble of positive energy." As you say these words, visualize the bubble around you. The specific words you use aren't important. Then forget the bubble and ask your partner to frown at you while he muscle checks you and your arm will come down. Smiles and frowns have an impact on our energy also. Now ask your friend to frown at you while you make the statement and visualize your energy bubble and have him muscle check you again. You will find that you are no longer weakened—or you aren't as weakened as you were before. Again, there is no magic here. Your mind is incredibly powerful. Focusing on a *positive idea*, such as a protective energy bubble surrounding your entire body, will be strengthening. You are literally creating a positive force that protects your body and your mind.

Your Seventh Energy Enhancer—Visualization

Visualization, the simple act of seeing something in your mind's eye, has many applications to help you counteract stress and take charge of your life. These techniques can also help you accomplish the goals you want to achieve.

Let's explore how visualizing works. Do this simple exercise:

ARM ROTATION EXERCISE

1. Stand up in a place where you can stretch your arms and rotate them without bumping into anything.

2. Keeping your feet firmly rooted in place, raise your

right arm up in front of you to shoulder level and, with your hand outstretched, turn your arm slowly to the right until you reach your discomfort point. Hold it there for a second, noting how far your body has turned and where you are pointing with your fingers.

3. Rotate back to the front and put your arm down.

4. Close your eyes and, without any movement of your body, *visualize* that you are raising your arm to shoulder level again, see your arm rotating to the right in a complete 360-degree circle with absolutely no pain or discomfort. Then visualize that you are returning your arm back to the front position and lowering it again.

5. Now, with your eyes open, repeat Steps 2 and 3, noting how much farther you are able to rotate your arm after the visualization.

Step 2.

Your body allows you to rotate farther after this visualization. In one study on the effectiveness of visualization, three groups of basketball players were tested doing dribbling, foul shots, and lay-ups. For the next two weeks the first group, which was the control group, did not play basketball at all. When retested at the end of the two weeks they were at the same level of proficiency as they were two weeks earlier. The second group practiced every day for the two week period; when they were retested, their scores went up. Meanwhile, the third group played no basketball but each day during the two week period they visualized as clearly as they could, seeing themselves doing the dribbling, foul shots, and lay-ups. When retested, this third group had the same proficiency level as the group who had actually practiced every day for the two-week period.

Many other studies confirm the fact that "seeing" an activity in your mind's eye, in as much detail as possible, has a profound effect on the body's performance of that activity. Many Olympic and professional athletes have been trained to visualize a gold medal. One example is Mary Lou Retton, a U.S. gymnast in the 1984 Olympics who was taught to visualize every step of her routine before she took her first step. She scored a ten on her last vault and won a gold medal.

Visualization can also be used to handle serious stress problems or to create important goals in your life. Here's how I once used it to help cure an illness. A week after I returned from a speaking tour to three South American countries, both of my eyes became bloodshot red. They were irritated and running all the time. After an eye examination, the doctor said I had an eye disease with no known cause, no known treatment, and no known cure. All he could tell me about this strange disease is that it usually went away in four to six months and it usually recurred.

I certainly wasn't thrilled with that diagnosis. In addition to the physical discomfort it was causing me, as a professional speaker talking on stress management, the idea of having bloodshot red eyes for four to six months was not particularly appealing. So I pulled out my nutrition books and I found that there are certain nutrients that are especially good for the eyes.

I put myself on a megavitamin therapy with nutrients such as zinc, bioflavinoids, and vitamin A. And I *visualized* twice a day as clearly as I could. In the visualization, I saw my white corpuscles riding in as white knights on chargers and zapping the red ones. This type of visualization technique is now being widely used by the medical community. Dr. Gerald Jampolsky has achieved remarkable success by using this type of visualization with children who have been diagnosed with terminal illnesses. He began the Center for Attitudinal Healing, based in Tiburon, California; there are now branches of the center throughout the United States. Dr. Jampolsky writes about this work in one of his best-selling books, *Teach Only Love*.[1]

After I did this visualization technique twice a day for one week, my eyes were totally clear. But then, a few days later, my vision blurred again. I went back to the eye doctor and this time the diagnosis was a virus that had infiltrated my cornea. He said it would take four to six weeks to get rid of the virus. So I went home again and both continued the megavitamin therapy and changed the visualization to match what I now had. Again, in one week's time my eyes were completely clear. I have not had a recurrence of either condition. I believe that both the vitamin supplements and the visualization helped to speed the healing process.

Energizing the World Around You

Smiles are a positive force. That's why it is so pleasant to be around happy, smiling people. You can get a lift, a sense of well-being, from being around people who smile a lot. These people are actually raising your body's energy level; and when *you* are smiling you are boosting the energy of those around you.

You can muscle check this by simply asking your partner to check you while smiling at you and when frowning at you. You will see and experience the same amazing results. The frown will actually weaken you, whereas the smile will be strengthening.

Next time you go shopping, notice the store clerks. Those who are smiling are influencing customers in a positive way and, as customers, we subliminally experience that message. We want to continue to shop at that store because it feels good. Customers may be less loyal to a store if the clerks are frowning, since shopping there leaves them feeling uncomfortable.

Recent research has even shown that a person's frown causes certain chemicals to be released by the body that have a negative, depressive effect on the person's immune system.

If you are in a situation where people are frowning, you can at least protect your energy system by using two of the Energy Enhancers mentioned earlier: the Energy Button and the Okay Sign. Doing these techniques will help prevent another person's negativity from reducing your energy.

Two recent magazine covers illustrate the impact a facial expression can have. Not all smiles are equal. One cover of *Esquire* magazine (March 1993) featured a photo of Roseanne Arnold in which her smile looked false. Another *Esquire* cover (April 1993) featured a pouty smile on Mick Jagger's face. Interestingly, the circulation of both of these issues of *Esquire* was lower than normal. Clearly these major stars believed they were being presented in the best possible light in these photos and it's a shame that that's not the case. If you want to dig up these magazine covers and muscle check them yourself, you will find that they are weakening, just as I did. In fact, I use muscle checking to be sure that everything from the typesetting on a brochure to the cover of this book is strengthening.

So put a smile on your face. It will really make a difference to you and to those around you.

A Word About Words

Did you know that your body responds to the words you hear? Words that your body/mind connection perceives to be negative are yet another drain on your life energy. One study showed that negative words suppress your immune system by lowering the white corpuscle count and the natural chemicals that protect us from disease and illness. We often use words or phrases without realizing they have this impact. For instance, if you stop to think about the phrase "I love you to death," it's pretty negative. Even though you consciously know that it is meant as a positive statement, your subconscious automatically reacts to any words that it perceives as negative, frightening, or stressful. Being loved to death is not a happy outcome. I'd rather be loved enormously.

Let's look at another word—*problem*. If you muscle check someone right after he says "I have a problem," the speaker will check weak. When the brain and body view something as a problem, it becomes more difficult for the body to function. On the other hand, if you muscle check someone after he says "I have an opportunity," he will check strong. Think about it: how would you feel if someone came up to you right now and said he had a problem? Would you jump for joy or would you prepare yourself to deal with something difficult and negative? Yet if someone comes to you and said he had an opportunity to talk to you about, you would be much more open and willing to listen and respond.

Try is another word that is perceived as negative by your conscious and unconscious mind. If you are asked to try to do something such as "try to pick up that ball," you subconsciously feel you must do it or you will have failed. *Try* infers that you will either win or lose. It doesn't leave you much choice. But if you phrase it differently and ask someone to "do his best," such as "do your best to pick up the ball," he won't feel he has failed if he is unable to complete the task. So long as the person gives it his best effort, then he can't fail regardless of whether or not he is able to pick up the ball.

Have your partner muscle check you after you say "I'm going to try to keep my arm up." Your arm will go down. Next say "I'm going to do my best to keep my arm up," and when you are muscle checked your arm will stay up. Other words that we have muscled checked and found to keep you switched-on: *do your best*, *attempt*, and *aim for*.

It'll be no surprise to you to learn that the word *test* has a weakening effect since we all grew up facing tests. The word *test* implies a pass-fail situation and that you are being judged. If I muscle check you after you say "test," you will check weak.

Throughout this book I have attempted to use words that will have a positive impact on you. For example, I refer to the muscle biofeedback system as *muscle checking* rather than "muscle testing." When you are being muscle checked, I want you to be clear that you are getting an accurate reading and not the impact of an outside stimulus such as the words being used.

I have had participants at my stress management seminars approach me to tell me how anxious they are to hear what I have to say. They mean they are excited but instead use the word "anxious." The word *anxious* tells the body that it should not be in a relaxed state. A better way to rephrase the statement would be "I am excited and looking forward to your seminar."

I suggest you begin to monitor your choice of words so you can begin to change negative words into positive words. Becoming conscious about your use of words is yet another way to switch-on your life.

Chapter 4

The Brain Switch: Educational Kinesiology

In the past few decades, a great deal of research has been conducted on the brain and its functioning. However, despite all of our advances, it is clear that the human mind is still a frontier which we are only beginning to map and understand.

One of the pioneers who is contributing to this understanding is Dr. Paul Dennison. Like Behavioral Kinesiology discussed in Chapter 2, the work of Dr. Dennison evolved in part from the concepts of Applied Kinesiology. However, Dr. Dennison's prime motivation was his work with children who had learning disabilities and problems with motor coordination. His research indicated that many of these problems were caused by a lack of integration of the two hemispheres of the brain. Dr. Dennison devised a system of learning and brain re-patterning which is now known as Educational Kinesiology (Edu-K).

The left and right hemispheres control different kinds of functions. The *left hemisphere* of the brain is the logical hemisphere, controlling skills such as language and arithmetic. It processes information piece by piece, logically, analytically, and in a sequential manner. The left hemisphere also controls physical movement of the right side of the body. The *right hemisphere* is the reflex or gestalt hemisphere. It has the ability to see the whole picture rather than the individual pieces. It is the receptive side of the brain and it absorbs and stores information gathered by the senses. The right hemisphere controls physical movement of the left side of the body. The two hemispheres are joined together by an area called the corpus callosum, which contains 200 million fibers that cross between the two hemispheres.

Before I go on, it's important that I clarify this concept further. While these functions can *usually* be attributed to the left and right hemispheres, medical science has discovered that neither side of the brain is *exclusively* related to any given function. In other words, there are exceptions to this rule. In general, however, the two sides of the brain carry out very different kinds of tasks.

When functioning in an integrated or balanced way, the two hemispheres cooperate and communicate with each other, giving us the ability to function smoothly in our daily lives. This is constantly happening as messages from the body are transmitted as electrical signals through the nervous system, to the brain, and then back to the body. For example, when you want to turn on a light switch, a message from the brain must be transmitted to the appropriate muscles which carry out that action. You must have the thought that the light is off and needs to be turned on. You must walk across the room, raise your hand to the switch, and push the switch with your fingers. A coordination of movements in both the left and right hemispheres is necessary for even this simple action to be carried out. If your hemispheres weren't integrated and communicating, you might end up stumbling over a piece of furniture or going out the door instead of turning on the light.

When you do an activity which requires both sides of your body to move at the same time, both hemispheres must cooperate and integrate for you to move properly. An additional boost to integration occurs when you do a movement that requires you to physically cross an arm or leg over to the other side of the body. This is called crossing the *midline* of the body. The midline is the center line of the body, running vertically down your body from head to toe. In effect, it divides the two sides of your face, the trunk of your body, and your legs into halves. The brain integration that results from crossing the midline can be very beneficial to your body energy.

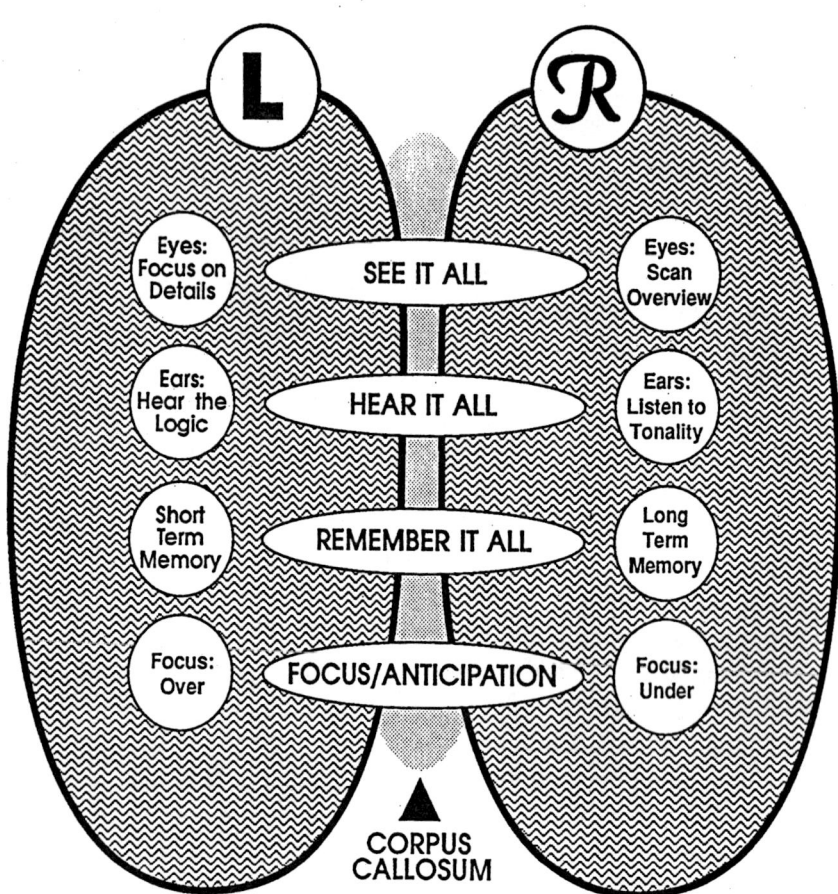

An example of lack of integration can be seen when a child with the learning disability called dyslexia is reading. As a dyslexic child begins to read on the left side of the page, he may have no problem. But when he gets to the right side of the page, he has crossed the midline and he suddenly begins reversing the letters because the eyes and the brain are not properly integrating the information being received from the right side. Some children (and adults, too) have unconsciously devised ways of compensating for this difficulty. An example would be keeping the entire book positioned on the left side of the body.

Our educational system has focused on the analytic approach, causing us to function primarily out of the left hemisphere of the brain. We have therefore become left-brain dominant and have switched off the right hemisphere when doing many of our daily tasks. In order to perform functions which are controlled by the right hemisphere, or things that require both hemispheres to cooperate, we must then switch-on the right hemisphere. Like a car that hasn't been started for a long time, the right hemisphere can be difficult to switch-on unless you know these Edu-K techniques. Performing right-hemispheric functions, therefore, as well as functions requiring both hemispheres to operate, is more difficult for some people.

To survive in the world, these people have developed compensating mechanisms to deal with this "one-brained" or homolateral approach to life. These compensating mechanisms may allow the person to perform the activities, but there is a price to pay; it may be more difficult or take longer to do the task. By predominately operating from the left hemisphere, a person will have "wired" these response into the entire body. Dr. Dennison's great discovery is that there are simple body movements called Brain Gym™ which we can do to change the wiring in our brain and re-integrate these functions back into both sides of the brain. These movement exercises allow us to bring the hemispheres into a *balanced* and integrated state. An activity such as reading across the page, which at first felt awkward, uncomfortable, and difficult for the child, can quickly become easy and fun through the use of Edu-K movements.

Brain Gym™

The various movements designed by Dr. Dennison have been correlated to the way we do different tasks, motor skills, and activities. One example of these simple movements is the cross crawl. (See *Illustration.*) To do the cross crawl you march in place, lifting each knee high. As you lift the left knee up, you reach across with your right hand and touch the left knee (or somewhere on the left leg). Then, as you lift your right knee up, you reach across with your left hand and touch the knee. When you cross the right hand over to the left knee, you are crossing the midline of the body and using both sides of the body simultaneously. This is called a heterolateral movement because both hemispheres have to cooperate in order to cross crawl successfully.

Cross Crawl.

Dr. Dennison calls the group of these simple Edu-K movements Brain Gym™ because it is an exercise program for the brain. Some Brain Gym™ exercises, such as the cross crawl, require movement; others are easy physical positions which are simply held for thirty to sixty seconds.

All of the Brain Gym™ movements were developed as a way to rewire or re-pattern the brain and the body from one-brained dominance to an integrated and balanced state; this balanced state permits the improvement of specific skills and attitudes. After nineteen years of "balancing" children and adults with Edu-K, phenomenal success stories have been researched and compiled.

Edu-K has also been recognized for its ground-breaking role

in education. In 1990 it was recognized as one of twelve innovative learning programs recommended to school systems by the National Learning Foundation (NLF), an off-shoot of the White House Task Force on Innovative Learning. Furthermore, it is one of only two systems recommended by the NLF in the area of mind/body work.

I have been personally teaching these Brain Gym™ techniques as a three-day course for a number of years now and have heard many success stories from our seminar participants. Schoolteachers who took the course and then implemented the system in their classrooms have told me of learning-disabled children who reversed their problems and were able to attend regular classes for the first time in their lives.

The near-miraculous results of Brain Gym™ is exemplified by this true story. A learning-disabled girl was starting the third grade. At the beginning of the school year, she was tested at a grade level of 1.9 in written-language capabilities. During the school year her teacher led her entire class through the Brain Gym™ movements for just five minutes each day. At the end of the school year, her improvement was dramatic. She tested at a grade level of 4.1 in written language. Usually an excellent improvement over a school year for a child with her learning disability would have raised her grade level by only two months, from level 1.9 to level 2.1. By using the Brain Gym™, she jumped more than two grade levels, to 4.1, in written language, and in every other area tested she also improved more than one full grade level. This child's improvement is typical of the results when Brain Gym™ is used in the schools.

Another success story came from a mother who went home after attending my seminar on Brain Gym™ and balanced her son on French and his little league batting average. Almost immediately his batting average jumped to 200 percent, and he went from a D to a B in French in one grading period.

Because Brain Gym™ is taught in a fun way, the kids look forward to doing the movements in the classroom. An art therapist at a psychiatric hospital said her children like to do the exercises because they said it gave their brains a "buzz." Even if Edu-K does not succeed at completely reversing a disability, it can help a person achieve his own increased level of ability and free him from feeling "stuck."

Edu-K Balancing For Goals

Edu-K is not just for kids. Dr. Dennison found that it could also be used in anyone's everyday life to release blockages and difficulties related to specific tasks or life goals. The participants in my seminar on Edu-K have used this system for a myriad of issues such as improving their golf games, getting exciting new jobs, losing weight, and even creating loving relationships. By using the Brain Gym™ movements, the negative programming that kept them from accomplishing what they wanted was released from their brains as well as their bodies.

Fear is a powerful force that can stop us from achieving what we want. Thoughts such as "What if I can't succeed at it?" and "What if I don't like it?" and "What will people say?" may be occurring at both the conscious and unconscious level. These fears can keep you stuck, while they influence your thoughts, attitudes, and even the level of enthusiasm you project to others. The Brain Gym™ movements can eliminate and release these fears and, at the same time, instill a positive pattern in your mind and body for creating the possibility of achieving the success you desire.

Edu-K allows us to focus on very specific goals; let's say, for example, you want to actually enjoy driving even in heavy traffic. You would do a series of appropriate Brain Gym™ movements which would integrate your entire system to be able to achieve those goals.

A while ago I used Edu-K to balance a writer on a screenplay he had written with his partner. I muscle checked Tony while he read the parts he wrote, and I found that his energy was switched-off. When he read sections of the screenplay that had been written by his partner, Tony muscle-checked in a switched-on mode. This result indicated that his partner's energy was balanced when he was writing, while Tony's was not. After we did the Edu-K balance, Tony's writing energy was also switched-on. The screenplay was sold to a major studio two months after we did the balance—and that was after five years of trying to sell it. Can we claim for certain the Edu-K balance made the difference? When you experience similar positive results over and over again after doing Edu-K balances, you will probably agree that Edu-K is a powerful tool to help switch-on our lives.

To her dismay, several years ago I found that Norma, my co-author on this book, was writing in a switched-off mode. Now, in addition to having used Edu-K balancing for her writing, she also plays hemisphere-balancing music (discussed in Chapter 6) whenever she writes, thereby insuring that the energy of her writing is always switched-on.

On a personal note, I can relate two very positive achievements in my life attributable to Edu-K balancing. The first is my happy marriage, in part due to Edu-K. Let me explain. I had been dating Marilyn for a year and a half. She wanted me to commit to getting married, which I had successfully avoided for forty-two years. I realized I was stuck on the idea of commitment. I used Edu-K to balance for the goal of being able to commit to the relationship and proposed marriage to Marilyn two weeks later. As the wedding date came closer, my commitment stayed solid and remains that way today.

The second story is about my parents. Whenever I telephoned or visited my parents, I always had the emotional and physical feeling of a wall going up, blocking me from feeling good and communicating well with them. After doing an Edu-K balance on this issue, the wall was gone and I found an immediate difference in my relationship with them. The wall has been gone ever since. Now I enjoy talking to them and visiting them. Marilyn has been amazed at the difference in my relationship with them.

I developed a course based on Edu-K brain-integrating techniques called Switched-On Selling. It's a one-day seminar for sales people using these techniques to remove the blocks they experience in the selling process. One example of what we address in the seminar is "cold calling." Cold calling is making sales calls to people the salesman doesn't know at all and who may or may not be interested in the salesman's product; they are a way of creating new customers. Cold calling is a major block for many people in sales. Because you never know if the person you are calling will be receptive, cold, or even hostile to your call, it can be difficult for many salespeople to get up the nerve to place the call in the first place. These salespeople who dislike cold calling may find themselves putting off making the calls by finding other things to do, such as cleaning their desks over and over again. For them, *anything* is better than the possibility of being rejected.

The stress of being faced with making cold calls can be debilitating. Some people fail because they just never get up the nerve to pick up the phone; others find a self-fulfilling prophecy occurs when they finally pick up the phone and the call goes so badly it confirms to them that they shouldn't have bothered to attempt the call in the first place.

The ability to successfully make cold calls can be the difference between succeeding or failing at a sales job. The brain integration techniques in Switched-On Selling help salespeople immediately get past these blocks. For example, an insurance company put only part of its sales force through the Switched-On Selling seminar. At the end of four months, when sales figures were compared between the group who took the course and those who did not, the seminar participants averaged 39 percent higher sales than their figures for the same period the year before, while the salespeople who did not take the course had sales figures that averaged the same as those of a year before. In addition, those who took the course were able to increase premium renewals by more than three times the rate of those who didn't take the course.

The success of the Switched-On Selling seminar has led to a seminar for managers called Switched-On Management. Additionally, I assisted Pam Curlee in the original creation of a seminar for golfers called Switched-On Golf. Pam's husband Paul, a doctor, was a mediocre golfer before taking the seminar. Now he's the proud winner of seven golf tournaments. A golf pro hit a hole-in-one after taking Switched-On Golf and then started teaching it to his students one summer. Out of thirty students, two hit holes-in-one that summer.

To put it simply—Edu-K works! You can change your life by balancing for goals through the use of the Brain Gym™ movements.

While I can't cover the entire three-day Edu-K seminar in this book, later in this chapter I will give you a number of the Brain Gym™ exercises, including a way to eliminate negative thoughts in your mind in just two minutes and a Seven-Minute Tune-Up which you can use as a way to focus and start your day as you integrate the hemispheres of the brain and balance your body. Feedback from people I've taught the Seven-Minute Tune-Up who do it on a daily basis have found that it has had an extremely positive impact on their lives.

Educational Kinesiology Muscle Checking

In developing Edu-K, Dr. Dennison used the same type of muscle checking as in Behavioral Kinesiology. However, he discovered that the hard, firm pressure used in BK was not necessary. He found that a much lighter pressure on the arm could be used just as successfully. The same muscle will respond even with one-fifth of the pressure used in BK checking. This was a very helpful discovery, since a person's arm tends to tire after a few rounds of BK checking. With the lighter pressure used in Edu-K checking, this tiredness is avoided.

Another difference in the checking method is that in Edu-K muscle checking the person who is being checked is the one who determines when he is ready for the pressure by saying "push." That tells his partner to start pressing. The word "push" is also stretched out to become "pusssssshhhhhhh" because doing so keeps the person being checked breathing. Otherwise there is a tendency for a person to hold his breath when the checker presses down, possibly altering the results. Here's how to do it:

Edu-K Muscle Checking for Normal Resistance

1. Face your partner.

2. Ask your partner to raise one arm up from the side

of his body so it is at a right angle to the body and level with the shoulder, with the thumb pointing toward the floor.

3. Place just two or three fingers of your hand above his wrist. Put your other hand on his shoulder.

4. Ask the person being checked to say "Pusssshhhhh" when he is ready and then lightly push down on his arm for about two seconds, using just a fraction of your strength. He should be able to easily keep his arm up. If you also look at his shoulder area, there should have been no movement taking place. If there was, it means you need to press more lightly. Repeat this light pressure several times. You now have a "reading" of the amount of pressure to use in Edu-K checking.

Edu-K Muscle Checking for Normal Resistance.

There are several things you need to be aware of when you are doing the checking. For example, when you cut a meridian line as we did on page 32, you may have the responses below:

- A person could be *recruiting* other muscles to help prevent his arm going down. To do this, he may tilt the whole side of the body up or raise the shoulder area up. If you observe recruiting, tell him to tighten only the shoulder muscle, which is called the deltoid muscle.

- A person could be a *fader*. When you press down with this lighter pressure, he may initially appear switched-on, meaning that his meridian line wasn't weakened; however, if you hold the pressure for a couple of seconds, his strength will begin to fade away and his arm will go down. It's important to press on a person's arm for several seconds so you don't miss the fader.

- The muscle may be mushy when you press down or the arm may not go down very far after cutting the meridian line. That's okay. With the lighter pressure you are only looking for subtle differences between switched-on and switched-off. (Remember, to get a clearer reading, you can do the harder BK muscle checking if you prefer, but the arm will tire faster.)

One of the things Dr. Dennison discovered is that our bodies can respond to us and answer yes/no questions. This is an exciting discovery that allows us to access the conscious and subconscious mind. It also allows us to confirm the positive changes we are making using the Edu-K movements. Follow these next instructions to determine the difference for yourself.

Edu-K Muscle Checking for Yes/No Responses

1. Follow steps 1 through 4 of Edu-K Muscle Checking for Normal Resistance.

2. Say out loud to your partner who is being muscle checked: "Your body will now demonstrate for me a *yes* response." Then ask your partner to say "Pusssshhhhh" as you muscle check his arm. His arm will stay up.

3. Say out loud to your partner: "Your body will now demonstrate for me a *no* response." Then ask your partner to say "Pusssshhhhh" as you muscle check his arm; his arm will go down. (Remember to be aware of recruiters and faders.)

As amazing as it is, the body now has the capability to answer specific questions. The person being checked or the checker can ask "yes" or "no" questions: "My body is switched-on to. . ." and name the issue he wants to muscle check. Then he says "Pusssshhhhh" and you push his arm down lightly. If the arm stays up, the body is saying "Yes, I am switched-on." If the arm goes down, the body is saying "No, I am switched-off."

Calibration or Pacing

Calibration or *Pacing* is a method of checking to see that the Edu-K muscle checking is totally accurate. When you have two pieces of scientific equipment being used in the same experiment, you must calibrate them to each other to make sure both pieces of equipment are measuring the same things. In Edu-K, Dr. Dennison has developed a method of calibration called Pacing. He found that if one person is not in calibration to the other, the person being checked may give what we call inappropriate responses. For example, if you say to the person being checked, "Your name is Susan," and she muscle checks "no" although her name really is Susan, you have an inappropriate response. Calibration prevents this situation from occurring. If a person being checked is weak on something that clearly should be strengthening, Edu-K Pacing gives us a method for correcting that imbalance so we can confidently proceed with the muscle checking.

In the calibration procedure, we muscle check a different meridian line from the ones I've shared with you so far. It is called the Central Meridian Line, and it runs from the belly button area to the area below the nose. We call this check "zip up/zip down." If the person checks inappropriately as discussed below, it means the person is over-energized. (See page 20.)

We also check the person's polarity to confirm that regardless of which hand I use to perform the muscle checking on my partner, I will get the same answers. We call this check the "polarity switch."

Finally, the Pacing procedure ends with a check for water. Our bodies are about 60 to 70 percent water. For chemical and electrical signals to be sent through our bodies, our systems must contain sufficient quantities of water. If you are dehydrated, interference in these signals can result. The calibration procedure to determine if the body needs additional water uses a method similar to one that was developed by veterinarians to check whether or not an animal is dehydrated. After all, you can't ask an animal how much water it's been drinking, so the veterinarian would pinch a bunch of the animal's skin together and then release it. How quickly the skin returned to normal would tell the veterinarian the hydration level. Since you don't want to pinch the person you are muscle checking, there is an alternate method: the person being checked pulls a piece of his own hair while saying "push," and you do the muscle check. If his arm stays up it means he has enough water. If it goes down, it means he is somewhat dehydrated. If the arm does go down, then both of you drink a glass of water and then repeat this muscle check by having your partner again pull his hair. Now his arm should easily stay up. We call this procedure "checking need for water."

Calibration/Pacing Procedure

1. Do the Basic Edu-K Muscle Checking Steps 1 to 6.

Zip Up/Zip Down

2. "Zip Up" by tracing a line with your hand from your partner's belly button to his nose. Ask your partner to say "Pusssshhhhh" and do the muscle check. Your partner's arm should remain strong and switched-on.

3. "Zip Down" by tracing a line with your hand from your partner's nose to his belly button. Ask your partner to say "Pusssshhhhh" and do the muscle check. Your partner's arm should be weakened and switched-off.

4. "Zip Up" again by tracing a line with your hand from your partner's belly button to his nose. Ask your partner to say "Pusssshhhhh" and do the muscle check. Your partner's arm should remain strong and switched-on once

again. If your partner's arm gives the wrong response on the muscle checking for the "Zip Up" (it came down when it was supposed to stay up) or "Zip Down" (it stayed up when it was supposed to come down), then stop here and do the Brain Gym™ movement Cook's Hook-Up on page 74. Then repeat Step 4. Your partner's muscle-checking responses should be appropriate now. Now proceed to Step 5.

Polarity Switch

5. Place your left hand above your partner's extended wrist and ask your partner to say "Pusssshhhhh" as you do the muscle check.

6. Place your right hand above your partner's wrist and ask your partner to say "Pusssshhhhh" as you do the muscle check.

7. Once again, place your left hand above your partner's wrist and ask your partner to say "Pusssshhhhh" as you do the muscle check. On Steps 5, 6, and 7 your partner's arm should remain strong and switched-on. If your partner's arm is weak on any of these three steps, stop here and do Brain Buttons on page 73. Then come back and repeat Steps 5 to 7. Your partner should be strong on all three checks. Now proceed to Step 8.

Need for Water

8. Ask your partner to pull a piece of his hair and say "Pusssshhhhh" while you muscle check him. His arm should be strong and switched-on. If his arm is weak, both of you should drink a glass of water and then repeat Step 8. Your partner should now check strong.

9. Have your partner repeat steps 1 through 8 on you. In Edu-K, both partners are paced because if either person's energy is inappropriate the responses could be affected. These steps are to be performed as the first part of every Edu-K muscle-checking procedure.

Calibration/Pacing Procedure

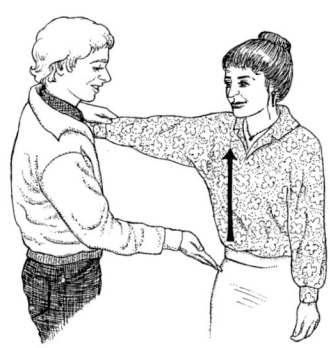

Step 2: "Zip Up."

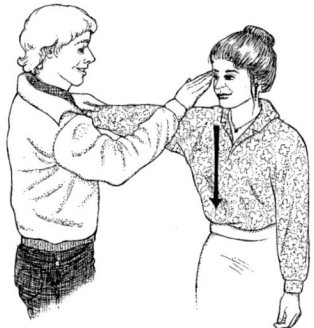

Step 3: "Zip Down."

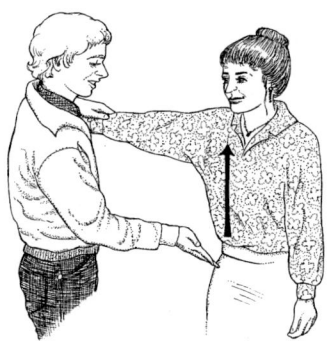

Step 4: "Zip Up."

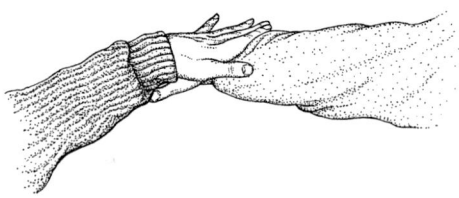

Step 5: Left hand doing Polarity Check.

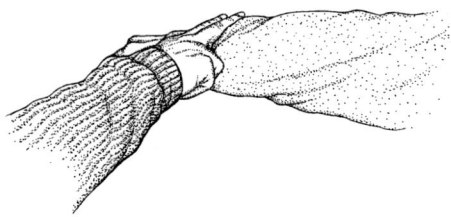

Step 6: Right hand doing Polarity Check.

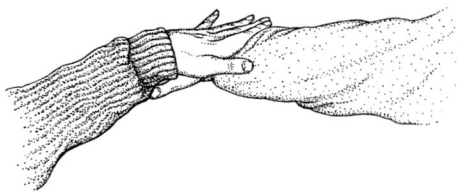

Step 7: Left hand doing Polarity Check.

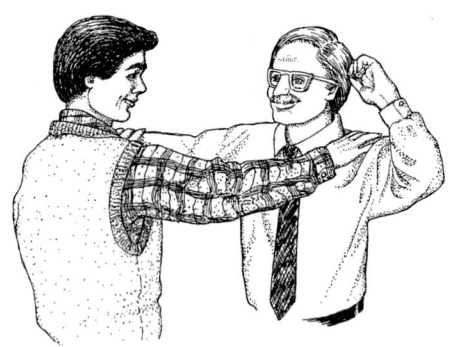

Step 8: Your partner is pulling a piece of hair while being muscle checked.

Self-Checking Methods

When it isn't possible to work with another person to do a muscle check, there are a number of self-checking methods you can use. At least one of these methods work for almost everyone and people find them just as reliable as muscle checking done with a partner. If these methods don't work for you, however, you'll need someone else to continue to do the muscle checking on you.

Self-Checking With Fingers

1. Place the tip of your thumb and the tip of your index finger of one hand together as though you are making an "okay" sign or a circle. Hold them together firmly.

2. Link together the index finger and thumb of the other hand inside the circle made by the first hand. You will be forming two links as in a chain. Just as in muscle checking your arm, you will first determine the normal resistance for self-checking. Attempt to pull your two circles apart. Don't pull so hard that the circles come apart; you want to maintain the thumb and finger connection without being able to break through.

3. Ask your body (silently or out loud) to demonstrate for you a *no* response and repeat Step 2. This time, the circle formed by the thumb and index finger should be easily broken when you pull the index finger through.

4. Ask your body (silently or out loud) to give you a *yes* response and repeat Step 2. This time you should be unable to break through the circle when you apply normal pressure.

Step 1: Form an "Okay" sign with your thumb and index finger.

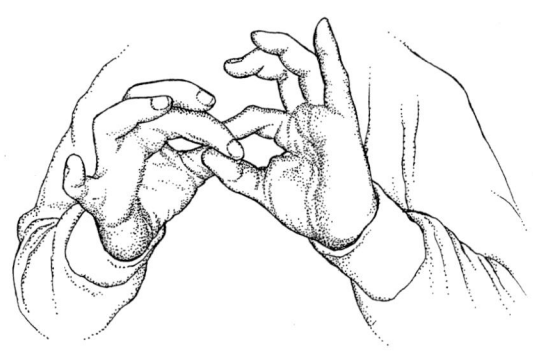

Step 2: Attempt to pull them apart.

Another self-checking method relies on *inner* reference points. To use this method, you will have to first establish "yes" and "no" responses from your body. You'll need to pay attention, as they may be more subtle.

Self-Checking With Reference Points

<u>To get a "yes" or switched-on response:</u>
Stand or sit quietly with your eyes closed and visualize or remember a past experience that was fulfilling and positive. As you recall this experience in your mind, become aware of an *internal* awareness that you can associate with this response in your body. Some examples of this internal awareness are:
- A feeling of ease or automatic movement
- A feeling of joy
- A physical sensation somewhere in your body
- A subtle movement
- A smile coming across your face
- A specific movement of eye, head, etc.

<u>To get a "no" or switched-off response:</u>
Stand or sit quietly with your eyes closed and visualize or remember a past experience that was challenging or created a feeling of being switched-off. As you recall this experience, be aware of an *internal* awareness that you can associate with this response in your body. Some examples are:
- A feeling of doubt
- A feeling of disappointment
- A physical sensation somewhere in your body
- A frown coming across your face
- A specific movement of your eye, head, etc.

Once you have determined this baseline for the internal experience of switched-on reactions and the comparable switched-off reactions of the body, you can check the body on any stimulus and ask it to give you a self-check *yes* or *no* response.

Positive Living Action Balance

We have all experienced negative situations. Many times memories of negative situations stay in our mind and eat away at us. With BK checking, you experienced the effect these negative thoughts have on your energy system. Although you can change your thoughts as you learned in the BK section, it is not a permanent elimination of the negative energy. You will need to continue monitoring whether you are viewing situations in your life positively or negatively.

Through the Edu-K work, you will learn how you can clear that negative energy out of your brain in only two minutes. Just follow the steps below and do the balance on your partner.

1. Do the Calibration/Pacing Procedure on page 64.

2. Ask the person being checked to think of a negative situation. She should visualize it with as much clarity as possible. When she has the situation firmly planted in her mind, ask her to say "Pusssshhhhh" and muscle check her arm. *If she checks strong, she is effectively dealing with this situation and there is no need to go further with this balance.* If her arm goes down, this is a situation that is draining and switching her off; proceed to step 2.

3. Ask the person to do Cook's Hook-Up (page 74) and Positive Points (page 75). As she is doing these positions, tell her to think of the negative situation negatively with as much intensity and clarity as possible. She will find, as she focuses on it negatively, that the negative thoughts will start to fade away or it will become harder to focus on the negativity. When that happens, tell her to start viewing the situation positively.

4. Ask her to think of the situation again and say "Pusssshhhhh" as you muscle check her. She should now be switched-on for this situation.

If you have been balanced in this manner and the situation recurs, re-triggering the negative thoughts, you can simply do the Cook's Hook-Up and Positive Points positions again while thinking of the situation negatively. Or, you may find yourself in that previous negative situation once again but you don't have any negative reaction at all. This latter response is what typically occurs from doing, even once, Cook's Hook-Up and Positive Points.

Seven-Minute Tune-Up for a Switched-On Day

These seven Brain Gym™ movements are very simple and yet profoundly effective. Doing these exercises every day will allow you to increase your energy and focus for the day.

1. *Drink a glass of water.*

2. *Breathe for relaxation.* Inhale through the nose while touching the tip of the tongue to the roof of the mouth just behind the teeth. Then drop the tongue and exhale through the mouth.

3. *Brain Buttons exercise.* While holding one hand over the navel, use the other hand to massage points just below the collarbone, to the left and right of the sternum. Do this for one minute. This movement stimulates the kidney acupuncture meridian line. It regulates the firing of neurotransmitters and increases the flow of the body's electromagnetic energy.

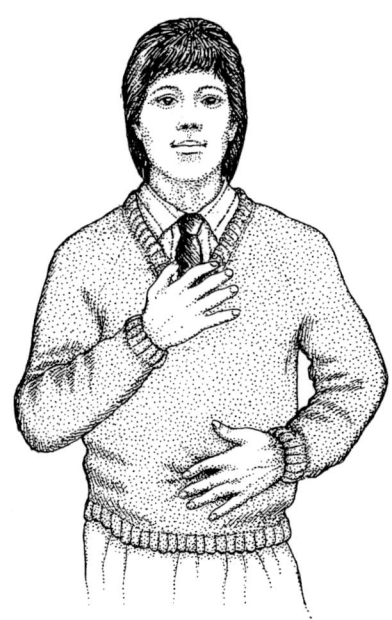

Brain Buttons.

4. *Cook's Hook-Up exercise.* This movement is done in two parts:

Part I. In a seated or standing position:
(1) Clasp your hands together and take note of whether the right thumb is on top of the left thumb or vice versa.
(2) Release your clasped hands and extend your arms out in front of you with the backs of the hands facing each other.
(3) Take the hand that had the thumb on top and raise it up and over the other hand; then intertwine the fingers of both hands together.
(4) Bend the elbows and bring the hands under and into the chest.
(5) If the right thumb was on top when you first clasped your hands together, cross the right ankle over the left ankle. If the left thumb was on top, cross the left ankle over the right ankle.
(6) Touch the tip of the tongue to the roof of the mouth just behind the front teeth.
(7) Close your eyes (if you are standing, keep your eyes open) and keep breathing. Hold 30 seconds.

Part II. Uncross your legs. Place just the fingertips of both of your hands together so they form a tepee. Keep your eyes closed and the tongue up and continue to breathe.

Cook's Hook-Up, Part I.   *Cook's Hook-Up, Part II.*

Cook's Hook-Up was developed by an expert on electromagnetic energy, Wayne Cook. Part I connects all the energy circuits in the body at one time and stimulates the movement of energy, if blocked. The fingertips touching in Part II balances and connects the two hemispheres of the brain. This exercise improves self-esteem and comfort levels in new situations.

5. *Hold your Positive Points.* The positive points are on the forehead above the eyes, halfway between the hairline and the eyebrow. You will find a little lump or protrusion on each side. It's in the vicinity of where the head curves. Hold these points with your fingertips lightly for 30 to 60 seconds. Keep breathing.

Positive Points stimulate the neurovascular balance points for the stomach meridian. Since much stress is held in the abdomen, this exercises deactivates the fight-or-flight response and allows accessibility to a new response to a situation. It increases speaking abilities and organizational skills.

6. Practice Integrated Movement. Close your eyes. Extend your arms out wide to the sides. Feel or imagine the left hemisphere of your brain in your left hand and the right hemisphere of your brain in your right hand. Bring both hands slowly together and feel the two sides of your brain coming together. Interlace your fingers and bring your hands in toward your chest in front of your heart while thinking and feeling "My brain is one."

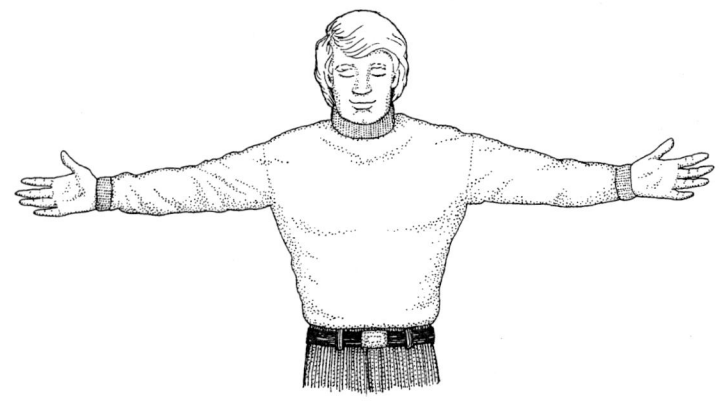

This is the starting position for Integrated Movement.

This exercise gives the body and mind the physical feeling of integration.

7. Do the Cross Crawl exercise. March in place like a drum majorette by coordinating your movements—when an arm swings up, the leg on the opposite side of the body moves up at the same time. It helps to touch the hand to the opposite knee. This movement makes you cross the midline of your body. *Variation of the Cross Crawl:* Touch the heel behind you with your opposite hand, being sure to keep the other hand to the front. Alternate opposite hands and heels to the back. You can also march touching heels in front of you.

The Cross Crawl activates both brain hemispheres simultaneously. It activates the brain for using visual, auditory, and kinesthetic abilities. This exercise improves listening, writing, and comprehension.

I've given you only a small sampling of the Edu-K material. Seminars are taught in the United States, Canada, and many other countries. If you'd like more information on seminars and books, contact the Educational Kinesiology Foundation at P.O. Box 3396, Ventura, California 93006-3396 (phone 800-356-2109 or 805-658-7942).

Chapter 5

Switching-On Your Diet

Food Sensitivities

In previous chapters we've used the muscle-checking procedure to determine which foods are good for an individual's body and which are weakening. Foods which are weakening to your system are foods to which you are allergic or sensitive. Numerous books on food sensitivities are available today; they alert readers to the myriad health problems that can result from eating common foods.

Symptoms of food sensitivities can be as debilitating as arthritis or as common as frequent headaches, digestive disturbances, depression, fatigue, irritability, and even problems with coordination, concentration, and memory. If the cause of the problem is a food sensitivity, it can be eliminated by simply taking that specific food (or foods) out of the diet. Certainly if you suffer from any of these symptoms, it is wise to look at the possibility that food sensitivities may be the prime culprit. Your doctor can do expensive tests to determine your food sensitivities. One commonly-used method, the scratch test, is painful and is actually not very accurate. Muscle checking is an easier way to determine what foods you may need to eliminate. It also costs nothing and there's no pain involved.

Unless you are tested for food sensitivities, you might not realize that frequently the foods to which people have detrimental reactions are the ones that are an everyday part of their diets. A person may actually be reacting to foods as common as wheat, eggs, soy, corn, tomatoes, cheese, dairy products, chocolate, and meats. These items are in many of the foods we eat. Wheat is in baked goods and pasta and is used as a thickener in sauces. Soy is present both as soy flour and soy oil and is a prevalent ingredient in our food supply. Corn is not just used as a vegetable; it is also processed into corn flour, corn oil, and corn syrup (used as a sweetener in many foods).

Once you have isolated a food sensitivity, it is important that you look for this food on the ingredient lists of all the foods you buy. You'll discover ingredients in packaged and processed foods that you would never have guessed. Be sure to eliminate any food that has an ingredient to which you have a sensitivity. Whenever possible, buy fresh foods and prepare them yourself. This is the best way to control the ingredients going into each recipe.

Use the Muscle-Checking Procedure on all the foods you usually eat to determine if you have a sensitivity to any of them.

Energizing Food

You may remember that one of the foods that is almost universally weakening is sugar. This does not mean you can never have sugar again. I still have an occasional serving of dessert. There is a method I want to share with you that will make you feel less guilty when you splurge on a food like this. This secret is what I call *energizing food.*

Take a package of sugar and do the following BK muscle check with it. (You can put a teaspoonful of sugar in several napkins or small envelopes if you don't have sugar packets on hand.) Although I'm using sugar in this example, you can substitute any of the foods which weakened you.

Energizing Food Check

1. Put the sugar in your hand.

2. Have your partner muscle check you while you are holding the sugar. You should check weak.

3. Now concentrate on the sugar, sending it positive energy. You can say a prayer to yourself or just think about the sugar being very positive to your system. It should take only a few seconds to accomplish this. Just a quick thought of energy or blessing is all that is needed.

4. Have your friend check your arm strength while you hold this packet of sugar. You will probably be surprised to find that the sugar packet is no longer weakening to you. Just to make sure that your arm is really strong with the sugar in your hand, have your partner check you again.

5. Now take a new un-energized packet of sugar and have your partner check you on it. Surprise! Your arm now goes down again. Since you did not send positive thoughts to this new packet of sugar, you did not change the energy level in it. It was your positive thought that actually *changed the energy level* of that packet of sugar you blessed or energized.

The idea that you can actually change the energy in a substance may be challenging for you to grasp. However, the same concept is at play when a magnet picks up a piece of metal. The magnetic energy causes the atoms in the piece of metal to form straight lines. We can't see this change in the formation of the atoms, but physicists have determined that this process is taking place. When the magnet is taken away from the metal, the atoms in the metal will stay aligned for a period of time, and then eventually the straight lines will break up. The same thing occurs when you project your positive thought: that thought hits and affects whatever you target. Since you weren't aiming at the un-energized sugar packet in Step 5, you didn't change its energy. This means you are uplifting the energy of foods by directing positive thoughts at them. The more focused you are as you energize your food, the more effective you will be.

Before I learned about the BK checking and the impact we can have on foods, I thought that blessing food before eating was a nice religious concept that had no real practical function. I thought it was just a ritual. Through muscle checking, I discovered that prayer is much more powerful than I ever imagined. You are actually changing the molecular energy of the food when you energize it through the use of positive thoughts or blessings. Kirlian photography (discussed in Chapter 3) also shows an increase in the molecular energy of food once it has been blessed.

You don't have to be religious to use this tool. Just sending positive thoughts will work. It will also work no matter what your religious or spiritual convictions are.

Due to the questionable quality of foods today because of added preservatives, chemicals, and sugars, blessing or energizing everything you eat is very important. Energizing takes only a few moments, and you can even do it silently without people around you knowing what you're doing.

Remember how the un-energized sugar in Step 5 still had a negative impact? Since you didn't bless it, you didn't affect it—even though it was the same substance as the packet you energized, and it was in the same room. You need to focus directly on the substance in order to change its energy level. This fact makes it important that you bless your entire meal. If the food is served in courses, then you can send your thoughts into the kitchen in order to positively raise the energy of the entire meal. This is clear from the experiment we did with the packets of sugar.

If you still have some doubts, here's a fun double-blind experiment you can perform.

Double-Blind Food Energizing Demonstration

You'll need two friends to take part; let's call them *Friend X* and *Friend Y*. Get several unused packets of sugar or envelopes containing sugar and write on the packets *A, B,* and *C*.

1. Muscle check Friend X and Friend Y on all three packets of sugar; they should be weak on all three.

2. Ask Friend Y to go into another room where he can't see or hear what's going on.

3. Ask Friend X to hold Packet B and energize that packet. Muscle check Friend X again and she should be strong on Packet B.

4. Now ask Friend Y to come back in the room. Muscle check Friend Y on all three packets. He should be weak on Packets A and C (the ones which were not energized) and strong on Packet B which has been energized by Friend X.

This demonstration shows that it doesn't matter who energizes the food. Packet B was not weakening to Friend Y even though he had no idea it was different from the other packets. Both of your friends will probably be astounded by this demonstration.

So, when you energize your food, be sure to send your thoughts to the food that's still in the kitchen. And remember to energize those mid-day snacks, too!

One thing I want to clarify: I'm not suggesting that by energizing the sugar you are making it into a nutritious food. You are certainly not adding vitamins and minerals to it when you energize it. But what you have done is to make the energized sugar more compatible with your energy system, so it probably won't be as depleting to your body as it would have been had you not energized it.

Now that you know how to raise the energy in a food, you are ready for yet another aspect of the incredible power of the mind and your thoughts. You can also *lower* the energy in a food simply by thinking negatively about it. So, hold one of the energized packages of sugar and think something negative about it, such as "this is terrible for me." Now have your partner check you again. Your arm will go down. You have just reversed the positive effects on the sugar and made it weakening again.

This same concept was observed in a study which was conducted with two groups of children. One of the groups liked spinach and the other hated spinach. The researchers analyzed the nutritional value each group absorbed from the spinach. The kids who liked spinach absorbed almost all of the nutrients contained in the spinach. The kids who hated spinach received almost no nutritional value from the spinach. The thoughts the kids had about the spinach seem to have actually affected the nutrients their bodies were able to absorb from the spinach. This study illustrates the fallacy of the "clean plate syndrome." Forcing children to finish eating foods they hate is not a switched-on way to add nutritional value to their meals.

When you do splurge and have that decadent dessert, remember to think only positive thoughts about it. If you energize it and then, half-way through eating it, have a case of the guilts and switch your thoughts to "this is terrible for me," the food will have lost the positive benefit of your thoughts.

The chef in a restaurant and the cook at home have a great deal of power to influence the energy of the meal. By cooking with love, they are changing and raising the energy levels of entire meals. When you eat in a restaurant that the staff and chef take pride in, you are more likely to have a positive experience.

Oh, by the way—don't forget the sugar that you de-energized. Bless it again and, in fact, bless all the packets of sugar. You can raise the energy in the entire cupboard of food simply by *thinking positively*. From some research I've conducted, I've found that a substance that has been blessed will remain energized for three or four days before the effect wears off and the substance returns to its previous lower level of energy.

You might be surprised that alcoholic beverages almost always check weakening. Think back to the time you had your very first drink of an alcoholic beverage. Your reaction was probably that it tasted terrible. The only reason you continued to drink was due to social pressure; your body eventually adjusted to the taste. This doesn't mean your body likes it; you just adjusted.

I once had a great time at a cocktail party with a group of international business people by using the BK checking and the energizing technique on glasses of champagne. The champagne was weakening for each person as I muscle checked them while they held it. Then I asked one of them to energize the champagne in his glass. I re-checked him and he checked strong. Then I asked a woman in the group to hold his "energized" glass and she was amazed that she too was now strong while holding it. Everyone was fascinated and amazed, while having difficulty believing what their eyes were seeing.

Another man then walked over to our group. He hadn't seen any of the BK checking and had no idea what we were doing. Without telling him, I put the energized champagne glass in his hand and he checked strong. Then, with another glass of champagne which hadn't been energized, he checked weak. Poor guy, he didn't even know what was going on!

Then I really upset the apple cart by whispering to one of them to focus negative thoughts on the energized glass of champagne. When I checked all of them again on this same glass of champagne, they all checked weak!

As you can see and experience, this concept concretely links the thoughts we think with results in our physical reality. It is incredibly powerful and, at the same time, it empowers us to take charge of our health.

Chapter 6

Switching-On Your Environment

It's probably clear to you by now that your energy is being affected by many variables that you were never aware of before. Let's look at some of the aspects of your environment, both at home and at work, that are impacting your energy and how you can switch these things on.

Lighting

Have you noticed that you feel more energetic when you go outside on a bright, sunny day? Rainy and cloudy days just don't give you the same "lift" that sunlight does. When people experience a couple of weeks of completely overcast days, they cheer when the sun comes out again. The reason is more than just psychological.

Natural sunlight actually stimulates your body's systems and functioning. Vision is only one of the ways the human eye uses light. Light entering the eye regulates and stimulates numerous autonomic metabolic and hormonal processes within the body, such as sugar balance, water balance, blood count, sexual function, and much more. If the entry of light into the eye is blocked due to blindness, then these metabolic and hormonal processes occur at a lower-than-normal level, and the body's natural day-and-night rhythm is also missing.

In the century since Thomas A. Edison invented the electric light bulb, few have thought that this marvel might have side effects that were not intended. But studies have proven that light can cause subtle changes in our health. This concept has become more apparent now that the majority of people spend a good deal of their waking hours inside buildings and school classrooms lit primarily by fluorescent lighting known as cool white tubes.

The use of fluorescent lighting is widespread because it is more energy-efficient than the incandescent bulb. A 40-watt fluorescent tube produces as much light as a 150-watt incandescent bulb. A fluorescent tube is filled with argon gas and mercury vapor. When a current passes through the tube, the mercury becomes excited and gives off a bluish light, or "fluoresces," when hit by the light.

For years, experts have been warning us that adequate lighting is essential for work efficiency and eye health. The belief developed that if a little light is good, then a lot of light is better. As a result, many buildings are now designed with lighting levels five times over what is needed—and they are lit almost universally by cool white fluorescent tubes. While we have been focusing on having the right *amount* of light, we have totally ignored the question of the effects of the light.

To show you the impact of cool white fluorescent lighting, we'll use the BK muscle check. You'll need a room lit by fluorescent lighting or a small desk lamp that uses fluorescent tubes to show you the impact. Ask a friend to help you while following the BK muscle checking procedure on page 18. First, have your friend close her eyes while you check her. She will check strong. Next, have her look directly at the fluorescent tubes while you test her arm. She will check weak.

The first research in this area was done by John Ott, Ph.D., a pioneer in the field of effects of light on health. Ott was originally a filmmaker who produced the early Walt Disney time-lapse films of flowers growing and blooming. In time-lapse photography, a frame of film might be shot once every thirty seconds while the camera is focused on a plant. This technique captures the entire growth cycle of the plant in a speeded-up fashion.

Originally Ott was hired by Disney to photograph flowers blooming. Since it was the middle of winter, he was forcing the flowers to grow in a greenhouse. They would grow fine, except that when it came time for the blooms to open, they would fall off. This process happened again and again.

Ott finally started altering the variables, such as the soil, water level, heat, etc. Finally, he put a colored filter in front of the lights shining on the plant. The plant bloomed magnificently. He then discovered that, by changing colored filters in front of the lights, he could get the plant to grow differently. For example, it might grow lush leaves but no flower, or it might grow long and spindly. Clearly these light and color variables had a dramatic effect. Some colors or combinations were beneficial; others were deleterious. Ott then turned to researching the effects of light on animals and then humans.

Ott has documented the ways in which the combination of light waves in typical cool white fluorescents adversely affects our systems in his books *Health and Light* and *Light, Radiation and You*. Ott's research showed that office workers reported feelings of sleepiness, despair, nervousness, irritability, nausea, and dizziness—all of which disappeared when lighting was changed to incandescent or to "full spectrum" fluorescent bulbs. He developed many theories connecting the absence of direct sunlight in our lives to such health problems as cancer, viral infections, and various eye disorders.

When full spectrum fluorescent lights were introduced into a work situation, Ott reported a variety of startling improvements. Industries have experienced a 25-percent increase in the productivity of their people by changing from cool white to full spectrum tubes.[1] In colleges, students' abilities to concentrate and to retain information have risen measurably; and in grammar schools, children who have been hyperactive have suddenly become calm and cooperative when the cool white fluorescent tubes were changed to full spectrum tubes.[2]

One of the reasons full spectrum fluorescent light is positive for the body is that it duplicates the natural spectrum of visible sunlight. However, just because a bulb is labeled "full spectrum" does not mean it is effective. I have performed muscle checking on a number of full spectrum bulbs manufactured by some of the major lighting manufacturers and have been surprised to observe negative results with some brands.

The only tubes I have found that muscle check very positively are sold by the company I list in the Appendix.

Unfortunately, full spectrum tubes are more expensive than conventional cool white tubes; however, they last many times longer than cool white tubes. When you begin to calculate replacement costs, the cost of the two types of tubes becomes comparable. And when you take health and productivity benefits into account, there is no comparison.

Research has also been conducted on a disease which afflicts people with cyclical mood-shifts called Seasonal Affective Disorder (known as SAD). Since 1984, SAD has been recognized by the American Medical Association as a distinct form of depression. SAD afflicts an estimated one million Americans, many of whom are undiagnosed. SAD is most prevalent during the wintertime, when people have the least amount of exposure to sunlight. The major symptoms that distinguish SAD from other types of depression are lethargy and overeating.

Though medical researchers are still searching for the cause of SAD, some theorize that it is caused by a disturbance in the body's natural clock and the resulting abnormal production of chemicals and hormones in the brain, interfering with the transmission of nerve impulses.

The most striking feature of SAD is not the symptoms, but the apparent cure. It is full spectrum fluorescent light. When a patient sits in front of a bank of full spectrum tubes for several hours a day, the SAD symptoms usually disappear within a few days. If patients discontinue their light exposures, symptoms return a number of days later.

Dr. Peter Whybrow, co-author of the book *The Hibernation Response* and Chairman of Psychiatry at the University of Pennsylvania School of Medicine, backs up the use of full spectrum tubes. Dr. Whybrow says people could dramatically change their wintertime moods by starting their days in bright light. His studies show that exposure to intense light, called phototherapy, can help cure wintertime depression. Of course, if you live in the north during the winter, you may find it difficult to get enough sunlight.

Another researcher, Dr. Norman Rosenthal, a psychiatrist at the National Institute of Mental Health, has shown an 80-percent success rate in a study conducted on SAD patients using full spectrum lighting as the method of treatment. Rosenthal says, "This light is correcting a chemical imbalance in patients' brains that manifests only when the amount of light they are naturally exposed to decreases."[3]

In addition to health benefits, companies have reported some very exciting results when they changed to full spectrum lighting in the work place, including substantial reductions in absenteeism and accident rates, marked increases in production, and significantly reduced complaints of headaches and fatigue. Studies on schoolchildren showed that after changing to full spectrum lighting, children had improved attention spans, reduced hyperactivity, and fewer days of absenteeism.

Let me share the results of a study, in which I assisted, at a hospital. We asked a group of nurses in the hospital to fill out reports during their workday relating to well-being and productivity. First we analyzed personnel while they worked under cool white fluorescent lights. Then, several weeks later, we switched the lighting to full spectrum fluorescent tubes.

The results of this study were dramatic. Fifty percent of the people had reported three or more headaches per week under the cool white tubes. When the tubes were switched to full spectrum lighting, not one person reported three headaches in any given week. Sixty percent of the people reported high levels of fatigue by four in the afternoon under the cool white tubes; under the full spectrum tubes, no one reported a high level of fatigue. Finally, 30 percent reported low productivity levels at the end of the day under the cool white tubes, versus 63 percent who reported high productivity under the full spectrum tubes after several months.

Hospital Study on Lighting

	Cool White *(Data collected before change to full spectrum tubes)*	**Full Spectrum** *(Data collected one week after full spectrum tubes were installed)*
Headaches per week	50% report 3 or more per week 20% report 1 per week 30% report none	0% report 3 or more per week 11% report 1 per week 89% report none
Fatigue Factor (by 4:00 P.M.)	60% report high level of fatigue 40% report small level of fatigue	0% report high level of fatigue 78% report small level of fatigue 22% report none
Productivity Level (by end of day)	30% report low levels 0% report high levels	0% report low levels 33% report high levels *(After several months under full spectrum lights, this figure increased to 63% reporting high levels)*

The most startling figure is the last one, on productivity levels. The swing from low productivity levels to high levels encompassed a 93-percent change in work-force productivity levels. Imagine: to compete more effectively with the competition, one of the easy things a company can do is to change its lighting to full spectrum tubes.

As a footnote, when the hospital changed back to cool white tubes, the levels of improvement disappeared. They immediately re-lit the entire hospital with full spectrum tubes.

Among the many reports I've received from clients who have found noticeable results from the change in lighting is this letter from Lynda Rinker, who is with the University of Wyoming Bookstore. She wrote:

> For several years employees have complained of sinus problems, dry eyes, headaches, etc. We had our heating and air conditioning filtering system cleaned and a more expensive filter installed, thinking our problems were being caused by a dirty system. However the problems persisted. Since replacing all of the bookstore's lights with the Excella [full spectrum tubes], headaches are almost nonexistent and dry eyes are a thing of the past. We noticed some improvement in our eyes almost immediately. The headaches were gone in a day or two. We have also had a lot of positive comments from customers. This is especially important to us since we are very customer-service oriented. We have no windows to let in outside light, so our customers' remarks about how bright the store now looks is a very positive comment.
>
> Our store is brighter over-all. Some of the comments from employees and customers are: "more natural"; "more like being outdoors"; "like them better and I think they have improved co-workers' moods"; "I love them"; "everything looked so yellow before."
>
> My headaches are gone and so are those of two other employees. I have also noticed I am not as tired at the end of the day. This is overall noticeable throughout the bookstore. Our employees seem more upbeat and positive.

Another client of mine, a real estate company in North Carolina, purchased a case of full spectrum tubes to experiment with in their office. The results were so positive that they re-lit the entire office and wrote me a letter saying this was the best thing they had done to increase productivity *ever!*

If you're not convinced that the added cost is worth it, then let me suggest the same strategy that I suggested to the real estate company. Just purchase a case or two from the suppliers listed in the appendix. Make sure you light an enclosed area because if you mix cool white and full spectrum tubes together you will lose the positive benefits.

Next, ask your people to keep records during the day on headaches, eye strain, fatigue, anxiety, productivity, accidents, illnesses, etc. Begin keeping these records while people are under the cool white tubes and collect the data for several weeks. Next, switch the tubes to full spectrum and have the people continue to keep their records. After several weeks switch back to the cool white tubes and watch what happens to people's scores.

By the way, the United States Environmental Protection Agency's new building is being lit only by full spectrum tubes. Does that tell you something about its benefits?

The results of this and other studies are very significant. Also remember your own BK muscle checking showed that cool white fluorescent lighting was weakening to your system. Changing the lighting in schools, offices, factories, and public buildings to full spectrum may be one of the single most effective things we can do to combat stress.

Color

Have you noticed that the color clothing you wear can influence your day? Putting a favorite shirt or blouse on in the morning may give you an uplifting feeling. One of the key things that makes that article of clothing a favorite is probably the color. Did you know that the color of the walls in your home or office can affect you? Colors are yet another variable in your environment which can be strengthening or weakening to your body energy.

Once again, if you follow the BK muscle checking procedure while looking at various colors, you will discover some colors are weakening to your body and some are strengthening.

You can do this BK check on various colors by having the person being checked look at different clothes, painted walls, and even samples of paint.

Remember the day-glow colors of the '60s? If you check day-glow colors, you will find that they are always weakening.

Years ago the television show "That's Incredible" featured a story on a police officer who lifted weights. It was easy for him. Then a pink board was placed in front of him and he attempted to lift the weights while looking at the board. He couldn't budge the weights at all! The only variable that changed was looking at the color pink.

Since that time, studies have shown that it's a particular shade of pink that affects people in this way. This color, which is now called Baker-Miller Pink, has been used in prisons, psychiatric hospitals, and youth detention centers to control violently hostile and aggressive behavior. Alexander G. Schauss, director of the American Institute for Biosocial Research in Tacoma, Washington, found exposure to this shade of pink lowered blood pressure, heartbeat, and pulse in an excited person.[4] Another study found, however, that aggressive prisoners put into a pink holding cell calm down initially, but if left there many hours they become even more aggressive. This finding indicates that colors need to be used wisely.

Other studies have shown that red walls in a prison create aggressive behavior in prisoners. When walls were painted a soothing color, this aggressive behavior was substantially reduced.

I was touring a mansion once with some friends. We entered one room that was painted sea green. One of the women said she loved the color and another said she hated it. I did the muscle checking on both. When I muscle checked the woman who hated it, her arm came down easily. Then I muscle checked the woman who loved the color. First I checked her in neutral and her arm remained strong. Then I checked her again at the thymus level by asking her to place her fingers on her thymus gland while she looked at the color. (See page 41 for the Thymus Check.) Again her arm stayed up, indicating that this color was actually creating energy for this woman.

It's a good idea to muscle check all the colors in your environment. This way you can make sure to switch yourself on to the colors that are strengthening to *your* system.

Music

The therapeutic uses of music are increasing daily. Soothing music piped through earphones in the dentist's chair helps to control the stress of pain and anxiety. Expectant mothers are told to bring uplifting music tapes to play during childbirth, helping to lessen the pain. Music has been effectively used to replace pain-killers and tranquilizers during medical procedures and as a treatment for stress-related illnesses, including high blood pressure, migraine headaches, and ulcers. Soothing music played during surgery reduces the need for pain-killing drugs during the patient's recovery. Researchers believe that some types of music trigger the production of pain-relieving chemicals in the brain, called endorphins.

But, of course, not all music is equal. Music, like everything else in your environment, can be beneficial or detrimental. Dr. John Diamond, the psychiatrist who developed Behavioral Kinesiology, found that most rock music (though not all of it) weakens the body's energy system. According to him, the weakening effect seems to be caused by a certain beat that is common in a lot of rock music called an *anapestic beat*. It is a rhythm of "da-da-DA," which repeats in such a way that the song almost seems to stop momentarily after each measure (after each "DA"). One theory in attempting to understand this is that this beat is contrary to our natural heartbeat of "lub-dub" and it throws the body's natural rhythm off.

Also, Dr. Diamond has found correlations between this type of sound and a phenomenon called *switching,* in which the left side and right side of the brain cease working together in balance. Many innocuous everyday activities can cause switching, as Diamond explains in his book *Your Body Doesn't Lie.* Switching results in one side of the brain working too hard. Thinking or solving problems becomes more difficult, and the person experiences increased stress. Since this is a typical state for many people, they don't notice these effects consciously, except for a vague sense of confusion, discomfort, or fatigue. The feeling may be "There's too much going on here," or "I have more demands on me than I can deal with."[5]

Not all rock music weakens us. For example, almost all the Beatles' music is strengthening except for the beginning of "Sgt. Pepper's Lonely Heart's Club Band," which has a heavy guitar riff. After that point it, too, is strengthening.

Check some music for yourself. Have a partner muscle check you for Normal Resistance. Then check again while you're listening to a particular record. You can check your whole music collection this way, to see which music actually strengthens you, which is neutral, and which music weakens you. If it weakens you, your arm will go down. If it is neutral, your arm will stay up; and if it is actually strengthening, your arm will stay up when you do the thymus check (see page 41). If music is played in your work place, muscle check some of the people there to see how it is affecting them. If it's weakening, perhaps you can change the music, or have it changed, to something that has a strengthening effect; check it and see.

Dr. Diamond cites the following example: "One factory in particular, a manufacturing and repair plant for sophisticated electronic equipment, where concentration and clear-headedness was essential, was playing a great deal of rock on its continual music broadcast system. It was recommended that this be eliminated. The management changed to different music and found to their delight an immediate increase in productivity and an equally pleasing decrease in errors, even though the employees were quite vocal about their dissatisfaction at having their favorite music removed."[6]

This anecdote illustrates the fact that people can become addicted to music that is unhealthy, just as they can become addicted to cigarettes and alcohol. From birth, we are exposed to so many things that are unhealthy or stressful that our bodies can become accustomed to the stresses and the state of disease and we actually wind up craving negative stimuli as much as or more than we crave positive stimuli.

However, people who begin to explore what would be healthy for them and start to incorporate these things into their lives generally find after a period of time that they feel better than they have ever felt in their lives. Their bodies become less confused and more instinctively sensitive to anything unhealthy, so much so that they find they may even be able to "taste" artificial additives or colorings in foods; they feel uncomfortable or ill when they eat or drink something unhealthy or find themselves in a smoky room; and when something in the environment lowers their energy level or dampens their spirits, they generally notice it immediately because of the contrast with their now-normal sense of well-being.

I recently came upon an interesting study that indicates that we're not the only creatures on the planet who are affected by music. Alicia Evans, a music therapist, measured the milk production in dairy cows during a study in which she piped four different types of music over stereo speakers into the barn. Classical music increased the output of milk by 5.5 percent. There was no change in the milk output of the cows when country music was piped into the barn. But when hard rock music, specifically the music of Kiss, was piped into the barn, the cows were reluctant to enter their stalls and their milk production decreased by 6 percent. The fourth music program wasn't music at all but included sounds such as clattering jackhammers and gunning car engines. When the cows were subjected to this "sound pollution," which many city residents hear on a daily basis, their milk production was even lower, decreasing by 12 percent.[7]

If you own or manage a business and you want to change the music (or the food served in the lunchroom or anything else that directly affects employees), the best procedure is to meet with the employees, explain and discuss the change and its expected benefits, show them the BK checking procedure, and make the change on a trial basis. People are much more likely to cooperate with this approach than with having change forced on them, even if "it's for their own good."

Some composers are aware of these energy concepts and use them to make sure their music is strengthening. One such composer is Steven Halpern, Ph.D., whose "anti-frantic" music is designed to be especially relaxing and energizing. In addition to his regular music, Dr. Halpern has a series of music compositions with inaudible positive statements designed to help you achieve successful changes in your life, including tapes for accelerating learning, weight loss, driving without stress, sleep, starting the day, effortless relaxation, peak performance, creativity, and health and well-being.

As an example, let me explain the way Dr. Halpern's "Accelerating Learning" tape works. You may have noticed that it is hard to stay awake when you read from a textbook or a thick technical report. At my seminars I ask, "Do you find when you open a textbook to study or a thick report to read for work, you immediately want to take a nap?" and the entire audience always responses "yes." On the other hand, when they read a good novel, they also respond that they can't put it down. The reason for this difference is that textbooks are almost always written by someone operating predominantly out of the left side of the brain; the brain energy is literally transferred into the words themselves and creates imbalances in the reader's brain hemispheres.

Playing Dr. Halpern's "Accelerating Learning" tape helps considerably. In my seminars, I demonstrate the benefits of this music tape by asking a participant to read from a textbook. Almost any textbook will do. While the person reads silently from the page, I muscle check him. The result is always the same: his arm is weak. Then, while I play the "Accelerating Learning" tape in the background, I ask the person to read silently from the textbook again. This time the arm is strong. Do a muscle check on a friend using the excerpt in the illustration on the next page and you'll get the same results.

Finally, a woman purchased Dr. Halpern's subliminal tape "Enhancing Your Self-Esteem" for her Attention Deficit Hyperactive (ADHD) 6 year old son. She had just taken him off of Ritalin and he was bouncing off the wall. She decided to play the tape twice a day. She also played "Accelerated Learning" when he studied. Until that point he had been "red lined" behaviorally at school every week. After the first week of having the Hapern tapes on, he was "green lined."

> The Prussian rulers believed that the Junkers made better army officers because they were brought up in the habit of commanding their own peasants. Bourgeois officers, a minority in all armies, were of the utmost rarity in Prussia. To preserve the officer class, legislation forbade the sale of "noble" lands, i.e., manors, to persons not noble. In France, again by way of contrast, where manorial rights had become simply a form of property, bourgeois and even peasants could legally acquire manors and enjoy a lordly or "seigneurial" income. In Prussia this was not possible; classes were frozen by owning nonexchangeable forms of property. It was thus harder for middle-class persons to enter the aristocracy by setting up as landed gentry. The bourgeois class in any case had little spirit of independence. Few of the old towns of Germany were in Prussia. The Prussian middle class was not wealthy. It was not strong by the possession of private property. The typical middle-class man was an official, who worked for the government as an employee or leaseholder of the large crown domain, or in an enterprise subsidized by the state.
>
> From *A History of the Modern World*, 6th Edition, by R.R. Palmer and Joel Colton (New York: Alfred A. Knopf, Inc., 1984).

Here's an excerpt from a textbook to use for your muscle check.

It is truly amazing how simple it is to balance the hemispheres of the brain and switch-on the body energy when we use the tools I am sharing in this book. (*Note:* In addition to certain types of music, the Edu-K exercises in the Seven-Minute Tune-Up on pages 73 to 77 will also help to integrate your hemispheres to stay awake and retain this left-hemisphere material.)

Another example of the positive impact music can have was demonstrated by a client of mine who owns a restaurant. He played Steven Halpern's "Connections" music tape for a half-hour every hour on the hour. He discovered that the amount spent per check and the tips to employees went up during that half hour and complaints went down.

Dr. John Diamond also has developed a series of music tapes which he calls "Biological Harmonics." These tapes were designed to reduce stress and anxiety while increasing your life energy. This series contains a careful mixing of biological sounds and sounds of nature blended together with carefully chosen classical music. If you cannot locate Dr. Halpern's or Dr. Diamond's music in your local stores, write to me for a catalog at the address listed in the appendix.

In addition to the inherent strengthening or weakening impact of a particular piece of music based on its distinctive type or category, the technology used in recording it has also had a role in the impact it has on the body. A number of years ago the music industry started to use digital recording technology for cassette tapes. Digital recording breaks the sound into millions of bits of electronic information. This process allows easier, more exact and more controlled editing because a single piece of a note from one voice or one instrument can be deleted, made louder or softer, speeded up or slowed down, raised or lowered in pitch, etc. Unfortunately, this advance in technology had a weakening impact on the body, although more recent advances have corrected the problems. Therefore, depending on the technology used in recording, some cassette music tapes have a weakening impact on the body when they are muscle checked, while others are okay.

By the time the technology for compact disks (CDs) came along, the quality of recording made additional leaps. Therefore, music recorded on compact disks (CDs) generally has a positive and strengthening impact on our systems. There are only a few exceptions, which can be determined by muscle checking. The same album of hard rock music that is weakening on a cassette will be okay when you listen to it on a CD. So if you are going to listen to hard rock music, make sure it's on CDs.

Electromagnetic Fields from Power Lines, Computers, Appliances, and Other Sources

For years, researchers have been studying the impact of electromagnetic fields on health. Electromagnetic fields have been found to alter electrical rhythms in the brain and influence behavior. Concerns about the health effects of electromagnetic fields have even led the Environmental Protection Agency to issue a warning. "The agency tentatively concludes that scientific evidence 'suggests a causal link' between extremely low-frequency electromagnetic fields—those having very long wave-lengths—and leukemia, lymphoma, and brain cancer. While the report falls short of classifying ELF fields as probable carcinogens, it does identify the common 60-hertz magnetic field as 'a possible, but not proven, cause of cancer in humans.'"[8]

The earth is surrounded by both natural and man-made electromagnetic fields. Our concern is about the man-made fields. From high-voltage power lines to the electricity running through your electric blanket, studies are indicating that there is good reason for this concern. The government first investigated the health effects of electromagnetic fields in 1979, when it found that Colorado schoolchildren who lived near power lines developed cancer at two to three times the national rate.

I did some muscle checking under high-voltage power lines. When a person stood under the power line, the electromagnetic field weakened the body and the person's arm came down. He had to move a distance of approximately one hundred yards away from the power lines for the body to no longer be affected. When I've muscle checked over buried lines, there was no detrimental effect.

What can you do to counteract your concerns about electromagnetic fields? When you have choice in the matter, follow the list of suggestions below. If you do not have a choice, then follow the other recommendations in the various sections of this book. Keeping your body energy strong will make it less susceptible to environmental effects such as electromagnetic fields.

Guidelines for Minimizing Effects of Electromagnetic Fields

1. <u>Power lines</u>: The high-voltage power lines that are strung along high towers carry electricity over long distances. Homes, schools, and businesses should not be built near them. The electric power lines that are strung along streets are lower in voltage. Nevertheless, studies have shown that we can be susceptible to the effects of these lines too. If you simply move your bed away from the outside wall of the house near the entry point of the power line you can lessen its negative impact. Burying power lines is the best option, even though it's the most expensive option, because underground they are no longer detrimental to us.

2. <u>Computers</u>: With computers we are concerned not just with the electromagnetic field but also the effect of the type of monitor being used. Turning the computer off when it is not in use and limiting your time in front of it

will lessen your exposure to the electromagnetic fields. Muscle checking has indicated that a computer screen called a VGA monitor will not weaken the body energy at either the neutral or thymus level. Comparing it with other types of computer monitors, the VGA monitor sends its signal to the screen in the same way that a television screen receives signals. It has a high resolution and uses an analog signal rather than a digital signal to transmit the information to the screen. I have found both CGA and EGA monitors to be weakening. If you already have a computer with the wrong monitor on it, you can purchase a VGA monitor for two or three hundred dollars. If you use a computer often during the day, it's a very worthwhile expense.

3. Television Sets and Appliances: Television sets, electric blankets, microwave ovens, electric ovens, clothes dryers, and other appliances all emit electromagnetic fields. Keeping a distance of at least five or six feet from your television set is a good rule to follow. Studies show that electric blankets interfere with the body's own energy system. If you use one at all, I suggest that you warm the bed with it and then unplug it before getting into bed and place a comforter over it to hold in the heat. Microwave ovens have been controversial for a long time with concerns about the powerful fields they generate. Limiting your use of any of these electrical appliances or staying away from them while they are operating will lessen the long-term impact of electromagnetic fields on your energy.

4. Bedside Clocks, Phone Answering Machines, and Tape Recorders: *Any* electrical source near your head is a potential problem; keep them all at least thirty inches away or, better yet, across the room.

The Positive Side of Electricity

While many scientists have a growing concern about the negative impact of electromagnetic fields on health, there is also evidence that electrical energy can be used successfully in therapeutic applications to promote healing. Dr. Robert Nash, a neurologist and leading researcher in the new field of energy medicine, says:

> There is a great need for knowledge of electromagnetic field bio-effects on human subjects, particularly in a therapeutic context of modulating and controlling biological rhythms and reestablishing disordered autonomic regulation. It appears that the USSR and Eastern Bloc countries have progressed substantially beyond Western countries in therapeutic applications of electromagnetic fields, ranging from psychiatric therapy to wound healing. Drs. Sitko and Zhukovsky of Kiev have over 125,000 case reports using resonant microwave energy devices.

Scientists have used electricity to heal broken bones faster. A slight electrical current is generated into a bone that is broken. It appears that the current causes the body to heal much faster than normal.

A machine that emits a slight electrical current, called a TENS machine, is used for reducing chronic pain such as back pain. When a patient wearing a TENS machine feels pain developing, he triggers the TENS machine to fire an electrical signal. The muscles in pain relax, and the pain is reduced or eliminated.

The Work Environment

In most work situations there are a number of variables that can be altered to maximize efficiency and productivity, lower fatigue, and generally switch-on the body energy. Remember the muscle checking we did in Chapter 3 on the spleen meridian line? (See page 33.) If the height of your work station or a physical movement you make repeatedly during the course of your day causes you to cut that meridian line, you will be depleting your body energy and be more fatigued by the end of the day.

Besides altering your energy system, a work station that is the wrong height for you can cause pain in your shoulders, back, neck, arms, and wrists. It is important to become aware of the factors in your work environment and, to the extent possible, make changes that will counteract energy-draining and muscle-fatiguing stresses.

Not making corrections can lead to long-term problems such as lower back pain or carpal tunnel syndrome in the wrists. The information below relates to how to reduce or eliminate these problems. This field of study is called ergonomics. The material below comes from the City of Virginia Beach General Services/Safety Office which I have adapted to incorporate BK muscle checking research.

Desk or Counter

The appropriate height for your desk should allow for you to have a 90-degree angle between your upper and lower arms as well as adequate leg room. If the desk is too low, you may be able to raise it simply by putting wooden blocks below each leg or corner. If it is too high, adjusting the height of your chair can make a big difference in your comfort level. If you work behind a counter most of the day and the height is incorrect for your body, check into ways in which the counter can be adjusted or your standing area raised.

Studies have shown that a small footrest, three or four inches high, can alleviate stress on the back as well as eliminate aches and pains in the legs and feet. Those who work standing behind a counter can benefit from resting one foot on the footrest, while desk workers have the option of resting both feet.

Computer Use

The height of your keyboard should allow your elbows to bend at a 90-degree angle when typing. If this angle is more than 15 percent higher or lower than 90 degrees, you are probably losing productivity and may be experiencing pain. Also, the keyboard should be elevated in the rear by about two and a half inches so your wrist can comfortably rest on the work surface. If your keyboard is not adjustable in the rear, place a book or piece of wood under it to elevate it to the appropriate level. You can place a wrist pad, which can be purchased from most computer stores, in front of your keyboard if an adjustment is necessary. We installed several in my office, and the staff noticed a really positive difference.

Your keyboard and monitor should be directly in front of you while you work so no twisting of the body is necessary in order to use it. An appropriate distance from the screen is 18 to 24 inches. If you are closer or farther than that you may experience headaches, fatigue, and eye strain.

Your monitor screen should be at a correct height for you; the top of the screen should be at eye level. If the screen is too low you will be forced to look downward, which causes muscle strain, fatigue, and stress. You can raise your monitor to the appropriate height by placing a book or piece of wood under it. It has been found that it is best not to have the screen tilted due to the glare from overhead lights or windows that results.

Glare on the screen can be responsible for fatigue and physical aches. When your screen is reflecting a lot of glare, you must constantly refocus your eyes and reposition your body to read the screen. Most monitors have a brightness control knob which you use to control any reflective glare on the screen. If you have adjusted the brightness of the screen and glare still exists, find the source of the glare and do what you can to minimize it. If the glare comes from outside windows, closing the blinds, even part-way, may do the trick. If it results from overhead lights, try taping a piece of cardboard to the top of your monitor so it overhangs by a few inches, shielding the screen from the lights. Or, perhaps you can move the computer or the desk to a different position to eliminate glare.

Because of the light being emitted from the monitor, those who work behind computer screens all day long are better off with an office lit slightly dimmer than usual. This reduction in room lighting will also reduce or eliminate reflective glare. Because we have all become so accustomed to extremely bright lights in the workplace, when you make the lights dimmer it may seem as though you do not have enough light. But once you are used to somewhat softer lighting, you will find it is easier on your eyes and your body energy. If needed, task lights can be attached to your desk. Just be sure the task light does not cause additional reflective glare on the screen. Another option in lighting is to replace ordinary fluorescent tubes with full spectrum tubes (as discussed earlier in this chapter). Clients of mine who have done so report reduction in glare from computer screens as well as a noticeable lessening of eye fatigue.

When you are working from a document, it should never be lying next to you on the desk, creating the need to constantly turn your head and refocus your eyes. Instead, purchase a document holder that will allow the document to be held in an upright position between the keyboard and the monitor screen.

Your Chair

An adjustable pneumatic chair is necessary for preventing poor posture. You should be able to sit comfortably in the chair with the soles of your shoes resting flat on the floor. At the correct chair height, your thigh muscles will be relaxed and your legs will not feel any undue pressure. The chair's backrest should also be adjustable and should maintain the normal arch of your back.

When you are working at a keyboard for long periods of time, your static posture can lead to cramped muscles. It's important that you take stretch breaks at least once an hour and more often if possible. Also, find little jobs you can do that will allow you to get up and move around. It may seem that interrupting your task is inefficient but, because getting up and moving around helps to relieve fatigue, it may actually boost your productivity. Also, short relaxation breaks can relieve muscle tension. Another option would be the Seven-Minute Tune-Up (on page 73) which will create that relaxation effect.

Other Workplace Stresses

Noise in the workplace can be very distracting. Simple things such as putting a cover over a noisy computer printer will help to control noise. Partitions between work stations also help to absorb noise and create a quieter working environment. Music played in the workplace can lead to productivity, but only if it is the kind of hemisphere-balancing music I discussed earlier in this chapter. Otherwise, it may be yet another stress on the body and the mind.

Additional Environmental Factors

In addition to those factors I've discussed in this chapter, Dr. Diamond has isolated many other factors in our environment which can be weakening to our life energy. From the gas emitted from a stove to auto exhaust, from industrial and household chemicals to synthetic clothing and bedclothes and the insulation in your home, there are many potential problem areas.

I'm not attempting to frighten you or make you feel powerless about your life. Rather, I hope you'll use this material and the muscle-checking concepts to identify the problem areas, change them if you can, and use the techniques on these pages to keep your energy switched-on.

Chapter 7

Switching-On Your Day

Now that you have all these techniques at your disposal, you might wonder how you're going to incorporate them into your daily life. Here are a few ideas on how to do just that:

Upon arising in the morning:

- Do the Meridian Line Strengthener. (The First Energy Enhancer; see page 35.)

In the shower:

- Do the Thymus Thump 15 to 20 times. (The Fourth Energy Enhancer; see page 40.)

Before breakfast:

- Do the Seven-Minute Tune-Up to set your energy level for the day. (See page 73.)

While preparing food, ironing clothing, working at a desk, or cleaning:

- Use the Energy Button by putting your tongue to the roof of your mouth. (The Second Energy Enhancer; see page 35.)
- Use the "Okay" Sign by putting your index finger and thumb in a circle. (The Third Energy Enhancer; see page 39.)

When you're grocery shopping or deciding what to make for a meal:

- Self-muscle check each ingredient to make sure your body does not have a food sensitivity to it. (See pages 69 to 71.)

Before you eat a meal:

- Energize your food. (See pages 79 to 81.)

When you think about a negative situation:

- Change your thought to a positive one. (The Fifth Energy Enhancer; see pages 42 to 44.)
- Do Cook's Hook-Up (page 74) and Positive Points (page 75) to get rid of the negativity.

While you're traveling to work:

- Use the Energy Button by putting your tongue to the roof of your mouth. Keep reminding yourself to do this throughout the day when you're not talking or eating, and it will soon become a natural position for your tongue. (The Second Energy Enhancer; see page 35.)
- Make the "Okay" sign with both hands by putting the index finger and thumb together whenever you're not gesturing or using your hands. (The Third Energy Enhancer; see page 39.)

To prepare for an important meeting, presentation, or test:

- Find a quiet place to spend a few minutes by yourself. Sit down, close your eyes and relax. Take a couple of deep breaths and start to visualize the meeting exactly the way you want it to go. See yourself walking into the meeting room, sitting down, making your presentation, getting comments and feedback. Visualize acceptance and approval from those at the meeting; see them agreeing to what you want and feeling great as you leave the meeting.

Do this visualization with as much detail and specificity as you can. (Visualization, the Seventh Energy Enhancer, page 45.)

When someone else is negative to you or when you are afraid or anxious about something:

- Use the Energy Bubble. (The Sixth Energy Enhancer; see page 45.)

Whenever you are upset, uncentered, or unfocused:

- Do the Cook's Hood-Up (page 74) and Positive Points (page 75), which help to release negative energy and negative feelings and allow you to center yourself again.

In the mid-afternoon when you are experiencing an energy slump:

- Do the Seven-Minute Tune-Up again to rev your energy so you can continue into the evening with energy to spare. (See page 73.)

Just before going to bed:

- Do Cook's Hook-Up. (See page 74.)
- Review the activities of the day. If anything negative occurred, do Positive Points (page 75) and you will be changing that energy.

Other Energizing Tips:

- Review your vocabulary and replace commonly used words such as "try" with words which are not weakening. (See page 49.)
- Replace regular fluorescent lighting tubes with full spectrum tubes. (See page 85.)
- Muscle check the color of walls and change to a strengthening color if necessary. (See page 92.)
- Play music that balances the hemispheres of your

brain for specific tasks, such as Steven Halpern's "Accelerated Learning" when you must read a technical report or a textbook and retain what it says. (See page 94.)
- Replace your computer monitor if it is not a VGA monitor.
- One more thing—Remember to have a great day!!

Appendix

Product Suppliers

Jerry Teplitz Enterprises, Inc., 1304 Woodhurst Drive, Virginia Beach, VA 23454. Phone 800 77-RELAX or 757 496-8008; FAX 757 496-9955; Email info@Teplitz.com. Supplier of books, audio CD albums and DVD's, full spectrum lighting, Steven Halpern's music. For a catalogue go to www.Teplitz.com.

Body Perspectives, P.O. Box 199, Clifton Park, NY 12065. Carries booklet on Kirlian photography complete with instructions and diagrams to build a Kirlian camera. Send $12.95 plus $2.00 S&H.

Star Industries, 11350 Brookpark Road, Cleveland, OH 44130. Phone 800-392-3552. Carries full spectrum lighting products.

Associations and Foundations

The Diamond Center, P.O. Box 381, South Salem, NY 10590. Phone 914-533-2158. www.diamondcenter.net. Contact for information on Behavioral Kinesiology seminars and literature and products.

Brain Gym® International, 1575 Spinnaker Dr., Suite 204B, Ventura, CA 93001. Phone 800 356-2109. Website: www.BrainGym.org. Contact for information on Brain Gym® and practitioners.

Energy Kinesiology Association, 834 Meadow Road, Severn, MD 21149. Phone 443-599-1113. www.ask-us.org

Suggested Reading

The Body Electric: Electromagnetism and the Foundation of Life by Robert O. Becker, M.D., and Gary Selden, 1985, Quill/William Morrow.

Brain Gym by Paul E. Dennison, Ph.D., and Gail E. Dennison, 1986, Edu-Kinesthetics, Inc.

Business Brain Gym by Paul Dennison, Ph.D., Gail Dennison, and Jerry V. Teplitz, Ph.D., 1994, Edu-Kinesthetics, Inc.

The Complete Guide to Your Emotions and Your Health, 1986, Rodale Press.

Edu-K for Kids by Paul E. Dennison, Ph.D., and Gail E. Dennison, 1987, Edu-Kinesthetics, Inc.

Health and Light by John Ott, 1973, Devin-Adair.

The Hibernation Response by Peter Whybrow, M.D., and Robert Bahr, 1988, Arbor House; 1989, Avon Books.

Life Energy by John Diamond, M.D., 1985, Paragon House.

Managing Your Stress: How to Relax and Enjoy by Jerry V. Teplitz, Ph.D., with Shelly Kellman, 1985, Happiness Unlimited Publications.

Personalized Whole Brain Integration by Paul E. Dennison, Ph.D., and Gail E. Hargrove, 1985, Edu-Kinesthetics, Inc.

Light, Radiation and You by John Ott, 1985, Devin-Adair.

Switching-On: The Holistic Answer to Dyslexia by Paul E. Dennison, Ph.D., 1981, Edu-Kinesthetics, Inc.

Your Body Doesn't Lie by John Diamond, M.D., 1980, Warner Books (also published under the title *BK: Behavioral Kinesiology*, 1979, Harper & Row).

Notes

Chapter 1. An Introduction to Switching-On

1. Robert O. Becker, M.D., and Gary Selden, *The Body Electric: Electromagnetism and the Foundation of Life* (New York: Quill/Morris, 1985), 242.

2. Emrika Padus and the editors of *Prevention* Magazine, *The Complete Guide to Your Emotions and Your Health* (Emmaus, Pennsylvania: Rodale Press, 1986), 569-570.

3. Padus, 570.

Chapter 3. Switching-On Your Life Energy

1. Gerald Jampolsky, M.D., *Teach Only Love* (New York: Bantam, 1983), 112-113.

Chapter 6. Switching-On Your Environment

1. John M. Ott, *Health and Light* (New York: Pocket Books, 1976), 114. Also published 1973 by Devin-Adair.

2. Ott, 192-194.

3. Montgomery Brower, "If Winter's Gloom Gives You the Blues, Norman Rosenthal May Be Able to Lighten Your Mood," *People*, January 11, 1988, 116.

4. Padus, 628.

5. John Diamond, M.D., *Your Body Doesn't Lie* (New York: Warner Books, 1980), 77-81. Also published under the title *BK: Behaviorial Kinesiology* (New York: Harper & Row, 1979), 40-43.

6. Diamond, 164-165; in *BK: Behaviorial Kinesiology*, 103-104.

7. Jeffrey Kluger, "Friendlier Farms," *Discovery Magazine*, March 1994, 38.

8. Philip Elmer-Dewitt, "Mystery—and Maybe Danger—in the Air," *Time*, December 24, 1990: 67-69.

9. Robert A. Nash, M.D., "Energy Medicine," February 14, 1990.

About the Authors

Jerry V. Teplitz, J.D., Ph.D., is a graduate of Hunter College and the Northwestern University School of Law and holds a doctorate in Wholistic Health Sciences. He is president of his own consulting firm and has been conducting seminars in stress management, employee productivity, and sales development for more than 20 years. He is also the author of *Managing Your Stress* and is a featured author in *Build a Better You Starting Now* and *The Stress Strategists*. Articles about Jerry have appeared in such publications as *Successful Meetings, Prevention,* and *U.S. Association Executives*. As a professional speaker, Dr. Teplitz has been honored by his peers in the National Speakers Association by receiving the title "Certified Speaking Professional," and he was selected as "Top Rated Speaker" by the International Platform Association. He has spoken to more than one million people. Dr. Teplitz is also listed in *Who's Who in America*.

Through his company, Jerry Teplitz Enterprises, a wide range of stress reduction, productivity and health-rated books and other products are available. They include:

> *BK: Behavioral Kinesiology* by Dr. John Diamond, the original book which introduced the public to Behavioral Kinesiology;
> Educational Kinesiology books by Dr. Paul Dennison and Gail Dennison: *Brain Gym, Switching On, Edu-K for Kids,* and *Personalized Whole Brain Integration*; and *Business Brain Gym* by the Dennisons and Jerry V. Teplitz, J.D., Ph.D.;
> *Fluorescent Lighting*, a report by Dr. Jerry V. Teplitz;
> Cassette Tape Albums by Dr. Jerry V. Teplitz, including *Managing Your Stress*; *Gaining Control of Your Future: Staying Younger Longer*; *Travel Stress: The*

Art of Surviving on the Road; and *Your Selling Success Formula;* DVD's by Dr. Jerry V. Teplitz, including *Instant Headache Relief, Par and Beyond: Secrets To Better Golf, Creating High Energy Websites & PR Materials* and *Power of the Mind.*

Information about seminars and products can be obtained by emailing, writing or calling Jerry Teplitz Enterprises, Inc., 1304 Woodhurst Drive, Virginia Beach, VA 23454; Phone 800-77-RELAX, or 757 496-8008; Fax 757 496-9955; Email info@Teplitz.com ; Website www.Teplitz.com.

Norma Eckroate has also co-authored *The New Natural Cat* and *It's a Cat's Life* with Anitra Frazier; and *The Natural Dog* with Mary Brennan, D.V.M. She lives in Los Angeles, where she works in television and film production.

BOOKS, TAPES, VIDEOS
CALL 800 77-RELAX TO ORDER

TRAVEL STRESS: THE ART OF SURVIVING ON THE ROAD (cassette tapes) - $85.00
This exciting six-cassette album with workbook is designed to meet the needs of executives, managers, salespeople and anyone who spends time "on the road". Dr. Teplitz shares with you his proven travel techniques gathered from his many years traveling as a professional speaker.

POWER OF THE MIND (video) - $85.00
Learn how completely powerful your mind is. Using your mind, you can actually create the things you want. Viewers will experience the difference between positive and negative thinking, how to change thought patterns, and the effects of music on the mind, body and performance.

INSTANT HEADACHE RELIEF (video) - $85.00
Just about everyone gets them. Now, there is a 4,000 year old technique which is both safe and effective called Shiatsu which eliminates a headache (or a hangover) in 1 and 1/2 minutes and migraines in 5 minutes. Shiatsu is actually a Japanese finger pressure technique for immediate pain relief. This video-tape also covers stiff necks, and shoulder tension.

HOW TO HAVE GREAT RELATIONSHIPS AT HOME AND AT WORK (cassette tape) - $50.00
Become a more dynamic, effective person in all your relationships both at home and at work. Learn Dr. Teplitz proven methods for: motivating others and inspiring their confidence; handling difficult people and gaining their cooperation; and getting the results you want when you give instructions or ask for something. The album includes a PERSONALITY PROFILE questionnaire and workbook that will give you important insights about yourself and others.

PERSONAL SUBLIMINAL MUSIC

This series of CD's was designed by Dr. Steven Halpern and contains a unique process, which uses music and inaudible positive statements to allow the listeners to achieve successful changes in their lives. Success is guaranteed or your money back.

CD's - $20.00

Achieving Your Ideal Weight
Enhancing Creativity
Sleep Soundly
Accelerated Learning
Enhancing Success
Effortless Relaxation
Stop Smoking
Enhancing Self-Esteem
Enhancing Intimacy
Attracting Prosperity
Accelerated Self-Healing
Caregivers Coping Skills
Radiant Health & Well Being

SUBLIMINAL BUSINESS MUSIC CD's

Success for Managers	$20.00
Success for Salespeople	$20.00

GENTLE MUSIC CD's

Connections	$20.00
Comfort Zone	$20.00
Message for Yoga	$20.00

To order or receive a copy of our latest catalog, or to receive a free monthly ezine, email us at info@Teplitz.com. To view our online catalog, go to http://www.teplitz.com and click on *Books-CD's-DVD's*.